# Cambridge Elements

Elements in the Philosophy of Søren Kierkegaard
edited by
Rick Anthony Furtak
*Colorado College*

# KIERKEGAARD'S *TWO AGES*

## A Literary Review

Lee Barrett
*Lancaster Theological Seminary*

CAMBRIDGE
UNIVERSITY PRESS

Shaftesbury Road, Cambridge CB2 8EA, United Kingdom

One Liberty Plaza, 20th Floor, New York, NY 10006, USA

477 Williamstown Road, Port Melbourne, VIC 3207, Australia

314–321, 3rd Floor, Plot 3, Splendor Forum, Jasola District Centre,
New Delhi – 110025, India

103 Penang Road, #05–06/07, Visioncrest Commercial, Singapore 238467

Cambridge University Press is part of Cambridge University Press & Assessment,
a department of the University of Cambridge.

We share the University's mission to contribute to society through the pursuit of
education, learning and research at the highest international levels of excellence.

www.cambridge.org
Information on this title: www.cambridge.org/9781009547413

DOI: 10.1017/9781009547468



When citing this work, please include a reference to the DOI 10.1017/9781009547468

First published 2025

*A catalogue record for this publication is available from the British Library*

ISBN 978-1-009-54741-3 Hardback
ISBN 978-1-009-54742-0 Paperback
ISSN 3033-4977 (online)
ISSN 3033-4969 (print)

# Kierkegaard's *Two Ages*

## A Literary Review

Elements in the Philosophy of Søren Kierkegaard

DOI: 10.1017/9781009547468
First published online: August 2025

---

Lee Barrett
*Lancaster Theological Seminary*

**Author for correspondence:** Lee Barrett, barrettl@moravian.edu

**Abstract:** This Element explores Kierkegaard's *Two Ages*, his literary review of a contemporary novella, situating it in the context of his other writings from the same period of his life and his cultural/political context. It investigates his review's analysis of the vices and virtues of romance and political associations, which he treats in parallel fashion. It traces a theme that certain types of both romance and political association can foster virtues that are necessary for the religious life, although the political ethos of his contemporary age mostly encouraged vices.

**Keywords:** Kierkegaard, *Two Ages*, political theory, philosophy of love, virtues



ISBNs: 9781009547413 (HB), 9781009547420 (PB), 9781009547468 (OC)
ISSNs: 3033-4977 (online), 3033-4969 (print)

# Contents

# Introduction: Kierkegaard on Romance and Political Community

In Kierkegaard's writings from 1846 and the surrounding years, a recurrent pattern concerning sociability, especially the possible religious value of romance and political community, can be discerned. This pattern defies easy assimilation to any standard ideological camp. A particularly fertile locus in which this pattern becomes evident is *Two Ages: The Age of Revolution and the Present Age: A Literary Review*, published in 1846 when Kierkegaard thought that he was concluding his formal authorship. While other writings from different periods of his life may suggest other patterns of relating Christianity and ordinary social bonds, this work limns a theme that pervades much of his corpus during this time span. It is also a theme that has been underappreciated and underexplored. We will concentrate on its articulation in *Two Ages*, situating it in the context of his other published and unpublished writings from this period of his career, roughly 1846–1848. It is not my contention that this was the essence or the culmination of Kierkegaard's reflection on these matters, but only that it was his attitude during a particular stage in his life. This is a snapshot of a way of thinking that was fluid and highly nuanced.

## 1 The Significance of Kierkegaard's *Two Ages*

## The Challenge of Reading Kierkegaard

Any corpus of writing as complex and elusive as Søren Kierkegaard's would inevitably spawn interpretive puzzlements and expository disputes. His pages are saturated with multiple voices, pseudonymous authors, thick irony, abrupt shifts in tone and topic, oscillations between ostensible humor and overt earnestness, and experimentation with hybrid genres. This kaleidoscope of literary devices was no accident, for Kierkegaard sought to destabilize the reader and force her to struggle to make sense of his texts. That interpretive exertion, he hoped, should vitalize the reader's struggle to make sense of her own life as she explored possible correlations between text and life.

Nowhere was this multivocity more apparent than in Kierkegaard's perplexing and seemingly contradictory remarks about romantic love and civic community. One of his pseudonymous authors, Johannes Climacus, quipped that, because everyone else had made life easier, the only thing left for him to do was to make life harder (CUP I, 185–87). In regard to making sense of romance and civic community, Kierkegaard succeeded admirably.

In his authorship and unpublished writings Kierkegaard wrestled implicitly, and sometimes explicitly, with the relation of the subjective dimension of religion, particularly Christian faith, to the more quotidian dynamics of human experience.

One of the most discussed ways in which he addressed this set of issues concerns the relations of the ordinary virtues of human sociability to the more demanding other-regarding virtues advocated by Christianity. Expositors of varying stripes have associated Kierkegaard's fragmentary social/political musings with almost every position found on the theological and philosophical spectrums. Some have castigated him for being the champion of a private, asocial spirituality, while others have lauded him for being an advocate of purified forms of intersubjectivity. Some have read him as positing a sharp disjunction of eros and agape, while others have seen him as merely wanting to purge human relationships of idolatrous pretentions. Some have construed him as a conservative monarchist typical of the cultured elite of Golden Age Denmark, others as an apolitical pietist, others as a populist champion of the "common man," and still others as an advocate for antinomian and transgressive politics. The fact that his authorship can sustain such a kaleidoscope of plausible interpretations raises the suspicion that Kierkegaard may simply have been confused, inconsistent, or erratic. However, in *Two Ages* a pattern becomes evident that is neither self-contradictory nor muddled.

## A Different Way of Relating Human Sociability and Christian Love

Kierkegaard used his literary review of a novella by Thomasine Christine Gyllembourg-Ehrensvaard (1773–1856) as an occasion to set forth his own reflections on the value of romance and civic communities. His remarks need to be located in a broad context, for they are an important subset of a larger set of issues. The significance of this topic is by no means restricted to social ethics, cultural critique, or political philosophy. The dialectical and often puzzling way that Kierkegaard delineated the interaction of Christian social virtues and more ordinary virtues can shed light on his more general strategy of relating the unique features of a religion, in this case the Christian faith, to other, more common dimensions of human experience. Kierkegaard's complex and sometimes controversial assessment of the religious significance of ordinary human sociality has major implications for the way that the purposes of ordinary human life and the religious life can be integrated (or not). Put starkly, the question is: Does religious subjectivity build upon, perfect, and complete the goodness of mundane life, or does it introduce an entirely new type of life, replacing the old?

Kierkegaard was the heir to a heated debate stretching back centuries, enacted dramatically in Irenaeus's polemic against the otherworldly Gnostics and in Augustine's disillusionment with the dualistic Manichees. Kierkegaard was very aware of the various attempts to resolve this matter from the theological lectures of H. N. Clausen (1793–1877) that he heard as a student.[1] By the

---

[1]  See Kierkegaard's notes in KJN 3, 28–66.

nineteenth century the issue was often conceived as the relation of the specific beliefs and values of Christianity to a general philosophical anthropology. A disjunctive and a conjunctive trajectory emerged, with many positions appearing in between the two poles.

One party stressed the distinctiveness of the language and culture of Christianity, seeing the religion as a comprehensive and self-contained paradigm for engaging life in general, differing from all other ways of constructing experience, and sharing no standards for comparison with them. Because of this irreducible singularity, proponents of this outlook often concluded that the values of a religion do not naturally grow out of any putative general features of human life. Consequently, there is no essential connection between the virtues of ordinary forms of sociability and the virtues of Christianity. Christian agape is not built upon natural forms of human sociality, nor does it perfect them.

On the theological side, in the early twentieth century Karl Barth (1886–1968) stated this position bluntly and extremely, denying that there was any "contact point" between Christianity and human experience,[2] and claiming Kierkegaard as an inspiration for this "qualitative distinction."[3] Much more recently theologians like Thomas Millay have discerned a disjunctive trajectory stretching from *Upbuilding Discourses in Various Spirits* through the "attack upon Christendom" writings and concluded that Kierkegaard was an extreme ascetic who regarded Christianity as being incommensurable with ordinary human self-regarding instincts and the forms of community based upon them.[4] On the philosophical side, interpreters of Wittgenstein have argued that there can be no general theoretic analysis of subjectivity, and therefore no account of the connections between a particular religion and the putative universal features of human life.[5] Because of Kierkegaard's aversion to sweeping metaphysical systems, many of these authors have regarded him as a harbinger of this suspicion of a comprehensive philosophical anthropology.

---

[2] See Karl Barth, "No!" in *Natural Theology: Comprising "Nature and Grace" by Professor Dr. Emil Brunner and the Reply "No!" by Dr. Karl Barth*, trans. Peter Fraenkel (Eugene, OR: Wipf & Stock, 2002).

[3] See Karl Barth, *The Epistle to the Romans*, 2nd ed., trans. Peter C. Hoskyns (London: Oxford University Press, 1933), 99.

[4] See Thomas Millay, *Kierkegaard and the New Nationalism: A Contemporary Reinterpretation of the Attack upon Christendom* (Lanham, MD: Lexington Books, 2021). According to Millay, Kierkegaard's call for the renunciation of the synthesis of faith and nationalism in his "attack upon Christendom" was an intensification of ascetic tendencies implicit in his earlier authorship.

[5] See Cora Diamond, *The Realistic Spirit: Wittgenstein, Philosophy, and the Mind* (Cambridge, MA: MIT Press, 1991); James Conant, "Putting Two and Two Together: Kierkegaard, Wittgenstein, and the Point of View for Their Work as Authors," in *Philosophy and the Grammar of Religious Belief*, ed. by Timothy Tessin and M Mario von der Ruhr (London: Palgrave, 1995); Stephen Mulhall, *Faith and Reason* (London: Duckworth, 1994).

The absence of such an anthropology would militate against any attempt to identify a connecting link between presumably universal human sociability and the sui generis mores of Christianity.

Other parties have seen religions in general, including Christianity, as sharing certain common features and ideals that are rooted in the depth dimensions of human existence. The natural virtues and modes of consciousness serve as foundations or springboards for religious experience and values. On the theological side, the exceedingly influential Friedrich Schleiermacher (1768–1834) inspired generations of "mediating" theologians who identified this depth dimension variously, sometimes as a sense of absolute dependence, sometimes as an intimation of a circumambient mystery, sometimes as a feeling of being gripped by an ultimate concern, sometimes as an encounter with the numinous, and sometimes as a moral imperative. Standing in this tradition, theologians like Arnold Come have claimed that Kierkegaard's exposition of Christianity relied upon a logically prior analysis of "humanistic" experience, including the intersubjective virtues embedded in that experience.[6] Therefore, the social virtues of a particular religious tradition, like Christianity, can overlap with, or even grow out of, natural forms of sociability. On the philosophical side, phenomenologists like Martin Heidegger and those influenced by him have argued that a highly general descriptive account of the dynamics of human experience *is* possible. If this is true, ordinary forms of human attachment could have some connection to Christian social values and norms. Perhaps agape is somehow founded upon eros, or is a refinement, an extension, or a perfecting of it.

Support for all these understandings of the relationship of general human experience to the specificities of Christianity can be found in Kierkegaard's corpus. These different strands in Kierkegaard's often knotty writings have been used to support different interpretive trajectories. More specifically, a case can plausibly be made that Kierkegaard saw continuities between general communal virtues and Christian love, and an equally plausible case can be made that he bifurcated them.

This Element will not attempt to resolve this pervasive textual tension in Kierkegaard's authorship as a whole. No single, monolithic pattern can be easily discerned running throughout his works. Rather, this exposition will concentrate on one specific instance of this seeming duplexity in Kierkegaard's writings: the possible relations of the virtues of ordinary social bonds to the communal and interpersonal virtues of Christianity. For Kierkegaard, the social ties of friendship, family, romance, clan, and political formations can harbor both positive and

---

[6] See Arnold Come, *Kierkegaard as Humanist: Discovering My Self* (Montreal: McGill-Queens's University Press, 1995).

negative implications for Christian traditions. I shall argue that Kierkegaard's complex and subtle treatment of this matter can provide insight into the more encompassing question of the relation of the unique discourse of a particular religious tradition like Christianity to the shared features of human life. But even this narrowing of attention is too expansive to be dealt with in a single volume. To bring added focus to this issue, we will concentrate on two forms of sociality that Kierkegaard treats in parallel fashion: romantic attachments and civil bonds, his twin foci in *Two Ages: A Literary Review.*

## 2 A Plethora of Interpretations: Kierkegaard on Human Sociability

### The Disjunctive Kierkegaard

Beginning with H. L. Martensen (1808–1884), Kierkegaard's former theology tutor and the subsequent primate of Denmark, many generations of Kierkegaard's readers have insisted that he contended that the virtues associated with natural forms of human attachment were heterogeneous with the values of Christianity.[7] Subsequent expositors like Theodore Adorno[8] and Martin Buber[9] intensified this critique, claiming that Kierkegaard was "acosmic," in that his understanding of religious subjectivity was hostile or at least indifferent to ordinary social goods. In the eyes of many readers Kierkegaard encouraged the suspicion that the "natural" virtues could contribute absolutely nothing to the formation of Christian faith in particular and the religious life more generally; in fact, they could only inhibit it.[10] According to this view, Kierkegaard believed that the bonds of romance, marriage, friendship, parental love, citizenship, partisan political attachments, and all forms of civic association, even at their best, are deeply defective by Christian standards.[11] Even worse, they are inimical to the individual's development of devotion to God and love for neighbor.[12] Along these lines, many scholars have concluded that Kierkegaard was drawing the same distinction of *eros* and *agape* that Anders Nygren (1890 –1974) would later popularize.[13] In recent decades Sharon

---

[7] Hans Lassen Martensen, Christian Ethics, trans. by Catherine Spence (Edinburgh: T & T Clark, 1873), 206–236.

[8] Theodore Adorno, "On Kierkegaard's Doctrine of Love," Studies in Philosophy and Social Science, VIII (1939): 413–429.

[9] Martin Buber, Between Man and Man, trans. by Ronald Gregor Smith (New York: Macmillan, 1948).

[10] See Karl Barth, Church Dogmatics IV, 2, ed. by Geoffrey Bromiley and Thomas F. Torrance (Edinburgh: T. & T. Clark, 1956), 727–783.

[11] See Sandra Lynch, Philosophy and Friendship (Edinburgh: Edinburgh University Press, 2005).

[12] See Knud Ejler Løgstrup, Opgør med Kierkegaard (Copenhagen: Gyldendal, 2005).

[13] Anders Nygren, Eros and Agape, trans. by Philip Watson (London: SPCK, 1953).

Krishek[14] and Daphne Hampson[15] have developed this theme in more nuanced ways in regard to Kierkegaard's view of romance and other "natural" forms of human attachment. Krishek has argued that Kierkegaard could have (and should have) proposed a more dialectical view of the natural loves and radical love for the neighbor, for he did develop such a view about faith in *Fear and Trembling*. Concerning political associations, Stephen Backhouse[16] has articulated a disjunctive interpretation regarding nationalism, as have Curtis Thompson[17] and Thomas Millay.[18]

These disjunctive readings of Kierkegaard are not fanciful in the least. The accusations that Kierkegaard bifurcated social goods and Christian values have significant textual foundations. Interpreters from Martensen to Hampson are surely right that Kierkegaard often did contend that Christian agape and more ordinary forms of love are drastically different from one another. Even more extremely, sometimes Kierkegaard did imply that Christian love for the neighbor is the opposite of the common forms of social relations. Many of Kierkegaard's writings do proclaim that natural attachments are not only the opposite of agape but are also impediments to it. For example, in *Works of Love*, written just a year after *Two Ages*, Kierkegaard argued that the natural loves are attempts to fill a lack in the self and obtain some sort of benefit from the other, whether that other is a human neighbor or God. Consequently, they are all reducible to forms of self-love (WL, 17–90). Kierkegaard did assert that romantic love and friendship are fueled by an attraction to some characteristics of the beloved that the individual desires, while Christian love is based on the sheer existence of the other. Unlike the natural loves, the endurance of Christian love is not contingent upon the continuation of the beloved's desirable qualities (WL, 52–53). Kierkegaard insisted that the natural loves are preferential, privileging some persons over others, while Christian love has a universal scope, treating all people with equal regard. He even asserted that Christian love for other persons is so

---

[14] See Sharon Krishek, *Kierkegaard on Faith and Love* (Cambridge: Cambridge University Press, 2015).

[15] Daphne Hampson, *Christian Contradictions* (Cambridge: Cambridge University Press, 2001).

[16] See Stephen Backhouse, Kierkegaard's Critique of Religious Nationalism (Oxford: Oxford University Press, 2011). According to Backhouse, Kierkegaard rejected the misuse of theological themes to support the alleged uniqueness and superiority of a national culture. Backhouse concentrates on Kierkegaard's exposure of the fictive nature of nationalistic identity constructions and self-aggrandizing ethnic histories.

[17] Curtis L. Thompson, *Kierkegaard Trumping Trump: Divinity Resurrecting Democracy* (Eugene, OR: Wipf & Stock, 2019).

[18] Millay argues Kierkegaard did much more than deconstruct nationalist myths, as Backhouse emphasizes. Rather, for Millay Kierkegaard is advocating a life of self-denial and the renunciation of the pursuit of power, for it is the desire for power that motivates nationalistic fervor.

unconditional that it does not even require reciprocity. Christian love gives itself away, needing and wanting nothing in return. Moreover, while natural love is dependent upon the vagaries of the lover's moods and interests, Christian love is impervious to the waxing or waning of the lover's enthusiasm. Kierkegaard warned that although the natural loves often promise eternal endurance, they actually are ephemeral and unreliable. Christian faith and love, however, are resistant to the corrosive vicissitudes of time. At times Kierkegaard suggests that self-loving desires must be repelled and renounced. Such a sacrifice would inevitably trigger the hostility of the social world that always recoils from discomfiting examples of self-giving.

A tendency to minimize the natural social virtues is also evident in Kierkegaard's account of love for God. Kierkegaard often warned that the natural tendency of human beings is to value God because some benefit can be acquired from God, and to trust God because there is some reason to expect that God can and will deliver such a benefit. These anticipated benefits often involve some sort of social fulfillment, such as contented family life, vocational success, national power, or public approbation. Contrary to this sensibility, genuine devotion to God is not contingent upon the expectation of earthly happiness and therefore is immune to the fluctuations of worldly fortunes. Many of Kierkegaard's upbuilding and Christian discourses castigate the impiety of thanking God only when circumstances are felicitous and prospects for social goods are promising (EUD, 90, 115). These dimensions of Kierkegaard's authorship do certainly seem to minimize or negate the spiritual significance of ordinary human hopes and fears, particularly social ones.

## The Conjunctive Kierkegaard

In the last few decades, however, other commentators have detected in Kierkegaard's authorship strong continuities between the natural loves and Christian love for God and neighbor. Epitomizing this interpretation, Jamie Ferreira has argued that agape particularizes and chastens the natural loves.[19] According to Ferreira, Kierkegaard's neighbor love must be concretized in different ways according to the specificities of particular relationships, and therefore presupposes the existence and value of natural social bonds. For example, neighbor love for one's spouse would be enacted differently than love for a needy stranger. In a different way, Natalia Marandiuc has proposed that Kierkegaard assumes that the extension of neighbor love to all humans is based upon already existing natural attachments, including attachment to the family.[20] John Lippitt has contended that

---

[19] M. Jamie Ferreira, *Love's Grateful Striving* (Oxford: Oxford University Press, 2001).

[20] Natalia Marandiuc, *The Goodness of Home* (Oxford: Oxford University Press, 2018).

Kierkegaard's analysis of *agape* functions as a "God filter" to purify the ordinary loves.[21] Most recently, Daniel Watts has claimed that Kierkegaard believed that the natural loves contain an internal contradiction, a self-regarding desire to be self-giving, that Christian love can resolve; in a way, Christian love is the fulfillment of the deepest drives of the natural loves.[22]

These interpretations, like those of the previous type, are certainly plausible and are indeed supported by themes in Kierkegaard's texts. In *Works of Love*, in spite of the warnings about the self-serving dangers of the natural loves, he did affirm that they could be reshaped and purified by love for the neighbor (WL, 375). Directed by the duty to love everyone unselfishly, the highly particular bonds of friendship, romance, and family, with all their special obligations, can become specifications of neighbor love, as long as the beloved is regarded first and foremost as a neighbor. (Of course, the problem remains that some relations, like familial ones, require preference.) Moreover, some of Kierkegaard's statements about the life of ethical duty suggest that the transition to religious subjectivity is not an abrupt "leap" but is rather a smoother, less disruptive transition.

Similar interpretive controversies concerning Kierkegaard's understanding of the relation of Christian virtues to political associations have been just as heated. Interpretive trends have waxed, waned, and resurfaced. In the late nineteen and early twentieth centuries, Kierkegaard was often construed as a precursor of political radicalism. After World War I, Kierkegaard was more frequently portrayed as being essentially apolitical, uninterested in the flourishing of civic communities. However, in 1980 Johannes Sløk departed from this standard view and portrayed Kierkegaard as a champion of enlightened despotism, in which all citizens know their place and function in society.[23] Jorgen Bukdahl[24] and Bruce Kirmmse[25] have challenged Sløk's interpretation and depicted Kierkegaard as an opponent of elitist culture and even as an advocate of egalitarian liberalism and populism.

None of these interpretive views have disappeared or been decisively discredited. All of them have contemporary advocates. Although some of them are vulnerable to the objection that they have illicitly generalized from a narrow swath of Kierkegaard's authorship, many are not susceptible to that critique. The troubling question remains: At any time in his career did Kierkegaard have a coherent and

---

[21] See John Lippitt, "Kierkegaard and the Problem of Special Relationships: Ferreira, Krishek, and the 'God Filter,'" *International Journal for Philosophy of Religion* 72(3) (2012):177–197.

[22] See Daniel Watts, "Love's Telos: Kierkegaård's Critique of Preferential Love," in *The Philosophy of Love in the Past, Present, and Future*, ed. by Natasha McKeever, Joe Saunders, and André Grahle (London: Routledge, 2021), 54–72.

[23] Johannes Sløk, *Da Kierkegaard tav: Fra forfatterskab til kirkestorm* (Copenhagen: Reitzel, 1980).

[24] See Jørgen Bukdahl, *Søren Kierkegaard and the Common Man*, trans. by Bruce H. Kirmmse (Eugene, OR: Wipf & Stock, 2001).

[25] Bruce H. Kirmmse, *Kierkegaard in Golden Age Denmark* (Bloomington: Indiana University Press, 1990).

somewhat positive understanding of the relation of the "natural" interpersonal and communal virtues to the social virtues of Christianity or any religion?

# 3 An Interpretive Alternative: Kierkegaard's Preparatory Virtues

## Virtue Pedagogy

The relation of sociality to Christian virtues (or the virtues of other religions) in Kierkegaard's work can be approached from a different angle. There is an underappreciated strand in his authorship and journals that suggests that Christian love for the neighbor and ordinary social relationships, including romance and politics, may not be as disjunctive as initially meets the eye, nor are they as conjunctive as some interpreters maintain. Unlike most interpretations of the conjunctive sort, this strand is not based on the possibility that love for the neighbor can emerge from, chasten, filter, or perfect the natural loves. Nor is it reducible to the possibility that an individual can reappropriate interpersonal relationships after attaining true religious selfhood. It is not equatable with the contention that certain forms of sociality provide the raw material that Christian love reshapes. It does not suggest that Christian love is an intensification of the natural loves. In addition to these themes in Kierkegaard's writings, whose presence cannot be denied, there is a thread that points to a different connection of romance and civic association to Christian virtues.

The exploration of this strand in Kierkegaard's writings relies upon an interpretive tradition that discerns in Kierkegaard's authorship an attempt to nurture (often indirectly) certain virtues that are presupposed by any authentic religious subjectivity, including Christian faith. The contemporary turn to "the virtues" as a lens through which to interpret Kierkegaard has arisen partly as an antidote to the tendency of existentialist expositors to depict him as a champion of punctiliar "leaps" that must be repeated *de novo* every moment. Alastair MacIntyre's rehabilitation of the virtue tradition in ethics, coupled with his critical assessment of Kierkegaard as an enemy of that tradition, triggered in reaction a spate of attempts to argue that various virtues are indeed central to Kierkegaard's project.[26] Contrary to MacIntyre, according to these interpreters Kierkegaard was a champion of certain virtues that were essential to his account of "inwardness." Robert C. Roberts, building upon the seminal work of Paul L. Holmer, has been in the forefront of this reconceptualization of Kierkegaard's moral and religious psychology.[27] In this interpretive literature "virtues" are

---

[26] See John J. Davenport and Anthony Rudd, eds., *Kierkegaard after MacIntyre: Essays on Freedom, Narrative and Virtue* (Chicago, IL: Open Court, 2001).

[27] Robert C. Roberts, *Spiritual Emotions: A Psychology of Christian Virtues* (Grand Rapids, MI: Eerdmans, 2007). See also Roberts, "Kierkegaard, Wittgenstein, and a Method of Virtue Ethics,"

described as perduring dispositions to entertain certain long-range goals, construe situations in particular ways, encourage certain passions and emotions in oneself, and act in certain ways. Virtues are not automatic products of an act of will, nor are they natural endowments of a personality. Rather, these sorts of dispositions require intentional cultivation in order to become long-term constituents of an individual's character. This highlighting of virtues and character is no alien imposition upon Kierkegaard's texts. Even though he seldom uses the Danish word for virtue ("*dyd*"), he clearly is absorbed with the long-term dispositions of the characters in the novel. Concerning the importance of the cultivation of intentional dispositions, Kierkegaard wrote a few months after he completed the literary review:

> Immediate feeling is certainly the first, is the vital force; in it is life; just as it is indeed said that from the heart flows life. But then this feeling must be "kept," understood in the same way as when it is said, "Keep your heart; from it flows life." It [immediate feeling] must be kept from selfishness; it must not be left to its own devices. (UDVS, 71)

## The Virtues in *Two Ages*

Kierkegaard's *Two Ages: A Literary Review*, rich in examinations of social virtues and vices, will provide much of the evidence for this interpretive project. In his review Kierkegaard explicitly associated the adherence to moral norms with the development of virtues and a cohesive, coherent character. He remarked that "Morality is character; character is something engraved...but the sea has no character, nor does sand..." (TA, 77). Character, the integration of various virtues, is that which gives continuity to a life, rescuing it from devolution into a sea-like flux or a congeries of grains of sand. Because of its unifying function, Kierkegaard identified "character" with earnestness about the shape and direction of one's life, adding pointedly, "Character is inwardness" (TA, 78). Although "inwardness" has many different nuances in Kierkegaard's various texts, in his authorial project here it suggests the cultivation of a unifying and enduring self-reflection and passionate self-concern in contrast to reflection's equivocation and common sense's shrewd abrogation of moral distinctions that reduces life to a series of "sorties."

Kierkegaard's authorship contains a strand that suggests that the natural loves can foster the development of certain virtues that can prepare an individual for

---

in *Kierkegaard in Post/Modernity*, ed. by Martin Matustik and Merold Westphal (Bloomington, IN: Indiana University Press, 1995), 142–166.

love for God and neighbor. In a way, they function as cardinal virtues which the virtues of love for God and neighbor presuppose.[28] For example, a person cannot love God faithfully unless that person has developed the virtue of fidelity. Kierkegaard echoed this theme in the occasional discourse "Purity of Heart Is to Will One Thing," published shortly after the literary review. Kierkegaard wrote:

> *Then everyone who in truth is to will one thing must be led to will the good,* even though it may sometimes be that a person begins by willing one thing that yet in the deepest sense is not the good, but probably something innocent, and then little by little is transformed into willing one thing in truth by willing the good. For example, sometimes erotic love has probably helped a person along the right road. He faithfully willed only one thing, his love; for it he would live or die, for it he would sacrifice everything, in it alone he would have his happiness. In the deepest sense, however, falling in love is still not the good but became a formative educator that finally led him, by winning the beloved or perhaps by losing her, in truth to will one thing and to will the good. Thus a person is brought up in many ways; an honest erotic love is also an upbringing to the good. (UDVS, 35)

Notice the explicit use of the concepts "formative educator" and "an upbringing" applied to romantic love. According to such passages, the growth of the virtues ingredient to genuine romance can serve as a preparatory pedagogy for Christian love. In these contexts Kierkegaard takes delight and comfort in the assurance offered by the novella that actual relationships (family, romance, friendship) can become spiritually significant (TA, 14).

This approach to Kierkegaard is not entirely new. In the late twentieth century Ronald Green and Theresa Ellis explored this possibility that according to Kierkegaard romance could be spiritually pedagogical.[29] However, the scope of their analysis was restricted to such texts as *Either/Or* and *Works of Love*. This interpretive trajectory can be extended by turning from these much-discussed volumes, which have been the scene of most of the interpretive fireworks, to an ostensibly less relevant text, the underexplored first part of *Two Ages*.

---

28 My account parallels that of Pia Søltoft in "On God, Passion, Faith, and Falling in Love," in *Kierkegaard's God and the Good Life*, ed. by Stephen Minister, J. Aaron Simmons, and Michael Strawser (Bloomington, IN: Indiana University Press, 2017), 31–45. However, she tends to stress that romance and Christian love have a common source, share common characteristics, and can be combined because of their shared desire to synthesize the temporal and the eternal, while I want to stress the ways in which the first type of love can be a propaedeutic to the second type.

29 Ronald M. Green and Theresa M. Ellis, "Erotic Love in the Religious Existence-Sphere," in *International Kierkegaard Commentary 16: Works of Love*, ed. by Robert L. Perkins (Macon, GA: Mercer University Press, 1999), 339–367.

## 4 The Unique Features of *Two Ages: A Literary Review*

### The Author, the Text, and the Reviewer

The novella that Kierkegaard reviewed, authored by Thomasine Christine Gyllembourg-Ehrensvärd, was published anonymously in October 1845 by her son Johan L. Heiberg (1791–1860), the dramatist, theoretician of aesthetics, publisher, and playwright.[30] In her son's journal she had already published several other anonymous short stories and novellas, the most significant being *A Story of Everyday Life*, which appeared in 1828. She was well qualified to reflect upon the political and romantic culture of the turn of the century's revolutionary age, for she had experienced it intimately. Her first husband, P. A. Heiberg (1758–1841), had been banished from Denmark in 1799 for his espousal of radical republican ideals. She divorced Heiberg and married yet another pro-French firebrand who was saturated with the salon culture of revolutionary period. This second husband, the Swedish baron Carl F. Ehrensvärd-Gyllembourg (1767–1815), was a political fugitive who had taken refuge in Denmark after having been implicated in the assassination of King Gustavus III of Sweden, an anti-parliamentary autocrat. Through her culturally influential son by her first marriage, an enthusiast for the philosophy of Hegel, she was also immersed in the more reflective spirit of the contemporary age. Madame Gyllembourg was no stranger to Hegel's fashionable aesthetics. Although Kierkegaard was not absolutely certain about the identity of the author of these stories (although he had strong suspicions), he appreciated the element of first-hand experience of both ages that was evident in her pages.

Kierkegaard had followed Gyllembourg's literary career avidly. In his review he wrote, "I have grown up under him [*sic*], and have not outgrown his influence." This was not the first time that Kierkegaard had paid tribute to this author (TA, 11). In 1839 in his first published work, *From the Papers of One Still Living*, a critical review of Hans Christian Andersen's (1805–1875) *Only a Fiddler*, he had discussed Gyllembourg's *A Story of Everyday Life* appreciatively (EPW, 76–91). Anderson was castigated for lacking a "life-view," while Gyllembourg was applauded for her ability to present a distinctive attitude toward life. Echoes of this earlier critique of Andersen and his lionization of Gyllembourg reverberate in his 1846 review. According to Kierkegaard, bad novels are trackless mazes without a life-view (TA, 18). An inferior novel suggests no possible explanation of life. He observed that the author's latest work expresses a developed, mature attitude toward life, and that the stories are the fruit of seasoned wisdom (TA, 14). The author, he applauded, had "won

---

[30] Thomasine Christine Gyllembourg-Ehrensvärd, *Two Ages*, ed. Johan Ludvig Heiberg (1845).

something eternal" by sketching the contours of an attractive and significant understanding of life in an appropriate literary form.

*Two Ages: A Literary Review* was written at a crucial point in Kierkegaard's career, a fact that suggests its significance to him.[31] While completing his monumental *Concluding Unscientific Postscript* he tentatively decided that he would not continue his career as an author but would restrict his literary efforts to the writing of reviews. By writing reviews, he thought, he would not be propounding his own views directly, but would merely be commenting on the thought and art of others. In a way, this would allow him to continue his strategy of indirect communication and the abnegation of authority that had been the reason for his use of pseudonyms. The writing of this lengthy essay was his first unsuccessful attempt to conclude his authorship and was symptomatic of a crisis in his self-understanding.

Another seismic event shaped the composition of the review. The infamous "Corsair Affair," his victimization by a scurrilous journal, raged from January to February 1846, while he was completing his slender volume, which appeared in March. During these months Kierkegaard was wrestling with the question of his vocational future in relation to his hostile social and cultural environment, whose harmful features were becoming increasingly obvious to him in a very personal way. The writing of the review was an occasion for the crystallization of his own reflections about himself and his culture much more than it was a tribute to the anonymous author.

The novella is a tale of two parallel romances, both set in Denmark, one in the explosive Napoleonic age of revolution and one in the contemporary bourgeois age of reflection. In both narrative strands the respective heroines, Claudine and Mariane, engage in an ill-starred romance, encounter an obstacle, and eventually enjoy a happy resolution of their love. In the age of revolution Claudine falls in love with a politically zealous member of the French legation to Denmark, Charles Lusard, who is then called away to a military assignment. Separated from her beloved, she flees to the countryside and gives birth to a child. In the age of reflection, Mariane falls in love with a financially comfortable but not extremely wealthy dilettante, Ferdinand Bergland, who hesitates to marry her because he fears that the union might lead to economic embarrassment. The contrast between the passionate and ideologically committed Lusard and the prudent and cautious Bergland, paralyzed by pecuniary anxieties, could not be greater. The pairs Claudine/Lusard and Mariane/Bergland are both archetypal representatives of their respective ages.

---

[31] See Joakim Garff, *Søren Kierkegaard: A Biography*, trans. Bruce H. Kirmmse (Princeton, NJ: Princeton University Press, 2005), 487–488.

## Romance, Marriage, and Civil Society in Kierkegaard's Denmark

Kierkegaard's *Two Ages* is particularly significant because it raises the issue of the pedagogical potential of romance for the religious life. The fact that Kierkegaard was drawn to a novella about romance was understandable, given the tensions in his culture, and given his terminated betrothal to Regine Olsen. During his lifetime Denmark was experiencing the pull of countervailing forces concerning the natures of romance and marriage. On the one hand, the valorization of marriage as a crucial component of a spiritually fulfilling life was still very much in the air. A generation before Kierkegaard, the still influential G. W. F. Hegel (1770–1831) had given this sensibility a sophisticated philosophical articulation.[32] According to Hegel, the abstract notion of ethical duty had to be concretized in specific social duties and roles, including marriage. Hegel's celebrated move from *Moralitat* to *Sittlichkeit* served as a justification of bourgeois familial institutions. The ethical person contributes to the well-being of society by being married and raising a civically responsible family. In 1841 H. L. Martensen asserted that the basic building block of society was the family, and that the foundation of the family was marriage.[33] Kierkegaard had been exposed to this theme throughout his childhood and theological education. For example, in Marheineke's Berlin lectures that Kierkegaard attended, Marheineke proclaimed that Christ had been born into a family and belonged to a state, thereby demonstrating the importance of both institutions for human flourishing (KJN 3, 267). In Kierkegaard's *Either/Or* the pseudonym Judge William epitomizes this conviction that contentment with life is achieved through the discharging of finite familial and civic obligations (EO II).

On the other hand, the value of marriages based mostly on economic convenience and the need to raise children was being challenged. Strands of the Romantic movement lionized the values of interpersonal and sexual intimacy in themselves, quite apart from marriage. Friedrich Schlegel's (1772–1829) controversial novel *Lucinde* of 1799 had invested romance and the freedom of the heart with the utmost significance.[34] Schlegel, at least in the popular perception, portrayed marriage as a repressive institution that stifled the creativity of women by trapping them in traditional roles.[35] Kierkegaard was well aware of this new ethos. In his

---

[32] Hegel, *Elements of the Philosophy of Right*, ed. Allen W. Wood, trans. Hugh Barr Nisbet (Cambridge: Cambridge University Press, 1991).

[33] Hans Lassen Martensen, *Outline to a System of Moral Philosophy*, in *Between Hegel and Kierkegaard*, trans. by Curtis L. Thompson and David J. Kangas (Atlanta, GA: Scholars Press, 1997), 299.

[34] Friedrich Schlegel, *Friedrich Schlegel's* Lucinde *and the Fragments*, trans. Peter Firchow (Minneapolis, MN: University of Minnesota Press, 1971).

[35] Katalin Nun, *Women of the Danish Golden Age: Literature, Theater and the Emancipation of Women* (Copenhagen: Tuscanum Press, 2013), 134.

thesis *The Concept of Irony* he critiqued what he took to be Schlegel's valorization of erotic pleasure (CI, 65). Even more, Kierkegaard condemned the polemic
against the institution of marriage, as if romantic love could only be erotic if it
assumed the form of adultery. For young Kierkegaard this was merely a reactive
form of immediacy, taking fleeting delight in breaking societal rules while being
doomed to ultimate disappointment. In *Either/Or I* Kierkegaard's pseudonym
portrays an aesthete who anticipates that the pleasure of an affair will be limited
and of short duration. In response to this sensibility, the dutiful civil servant and
family man Judge William continuously warns that eroticism cannot satisfy the
infinite nature of human desire (EO II). However, the judge's ponderous, moral-
izing, and often self-satisfied tone undercuts his encomiums to marriage s alleged
integration of passion and duty. The fact that the life of neither character is
completely attractive displays Kierkegaard's dissatisfaction with the major contemporary understandings of romance and marriage.

The review is also significant because it raises the question of the religious
value of sociality not only regarding romance, but also regarding political life.
Most importantly it treats the two types of relationality in a parallel and
interactive fashion. Taken together, the micro-analysis of romance and the
macro-analysis of the cultural/political sphere provide a blueprint for the
interpretation of other social phenomena. Kierkegaard does not analyze friendship, parent–child relations, or informal clubs in any detail, but the consider-
ations that he articulates could be applied to them. His evaluative tools are
transferrable, with some modification, to most other social formations.

## The Significance of a Life-View

Kierkegaard's praise for the author's literary career is based on its manifestation of
a coherent, consistent "life-view," exemplified by the two heroines in her latest
novella. That life-view, appearing in different guises in the two different ages, is
essentially the same in the two contexts, despite the differences in ethos. For
Kierkegaard a "life-view" is a comprehensive stance toward an individual's existence as a whole. It is a distinctive way of acting, feeling, desiring, and thinking,
a unique style of integrating and giving meaning to the diverse components of
a life. With a coherent life-view in place, a pervasive demeanor informs everything
that an individual does and undergoes. Life-views are long-term characterizations
of a person, forging the discrete episodes and aspects of a life into a unity, both
diachronically and synchronically. Because they encourage perduring dispositions
that fit together, life-views can be regarded as integrated networks of virtues.

In Kierkegaard's estimation, the corpus of this author earns high marks in the
life-view department. All serious novels, he asserted, should exhibit a life-view,

and the composite literary production of an author should exhibit a consistent life-view over time. Kierkegaard exulted that this anonymous author has indeed remained true to her life-view throughout her authorship, from her earlier *Story of Everyday Life* to *Two Ages*. In his review Kierkegaard emphasized the existential importance of the continuity in the author's adherence to this distinctive life-view. In her books, he wrote, "the disquietude is essentially the same, the quietude is essentially the same, the movement in all the stories is essentially from the same to the same; the discord introduced has essentially the same resilience, the peacefulness and relaxation are also the same – that is, the life-view is the same" (TA, 14). Kierkegaard frequently repeats that the life-view that sustains the main characters through their tribulations and joys is enduring. Plaudits are due to the author not primarily because the literary artistry and style have been consistent, but because her wisdom about life has been consistent. The author, he exclaimed, has remained true to herself, even though the world and cultural tastes had changed during her writing career (TA, 8). Changeableness in an author is symptomatic of having no internal values that give direction and continuity to a life (TA, 8); it is having "the law of existence outside yourself" (TA, 7). Contrary to this, a life-view should persist despite the fluctuating demands of the times, a virtue that this author exemplifies. This consistency catapults her works into the category of texts from which a reader can learn something significant about life.

Kierkegaard reinforces the theme of the importance of the continuity of a life-view by applying it to himself as a reviewer. He hopes that he, the reviewer, has remained unchanged from his assessment of the author in 1836 to his current review in 1845. Even better, he hopes that if he has changed, he has changed by becoming "a little clearer," with "more inwardness, non-identical repetition" (TA, 23). Moreover, he trusts that the public has remained faithful to the author, as the author's continuing popularity suggests (TA, 16). These instances of changelessness on the part of the author, the reviewer, and the reading public are essentially examples of the continuing attraction of an ideal view of life.

Kierkegaard compared these triple examples of life-view continuities to the constancy of ethical commitments. The ethical dimensions of the stories must be granted predominance over the variable demands of the times (TA, 8). Adding a religious modulation, Kierkegaard identified this ethical dimension with the quiet divine voice of conscience. He warned that "the voice of God is always a whisper, while the demand of the age is a thousand-tongued rumor, not an all-powerful call that creates great men but a stirring in the offal" (TA, 10). Although it is a whisper, the imperative dimension of a life-view not only supports the changelessness of an individual, but also unifies the self at every present moment in resistance to the disintegrating and fluctuating forces of the contemporary age.

## An Appreciation of Romance and Civic Community

The specific life-view presented here is unusual in Kierkegaard's corpus. It does not fit neatly into the categories of the "stages" (aesthetic ethical, religious, Christian) that were canonized and ossified by earlier generations of Kierkegaard scholars. It diverges sharply from the ways of life that he or his pseudonyms describe elsewhere, such as the life of duty or the life of infinite resignation. Surprisingly, this review is Kierkegaard's panegyric to a certain kind of romance, something that one would not expect to find in Kierkegaard's signed authorship. Here, romance is presented in a much more favorable light than it is in his other texts. The unusual point of his review is that certain kinds of romance can form individuals in spiritually beneficial ways.

A second, perhaps even more surprising, theme is suggested by the review. Given the parallelism of the cultural/political sphere and the romantic sphere, Kierkegaard's approval of certain aspects of romance in the private sphere suggests that beneficial aspects can also be found the more public forms of association (TA, 32). His approbative attitude toward the romances depicted in the novella has implications for the forms of association that constitute the public sphere. To anticipate my conclusion: not only does romance encourage some virtues that can serve as a propaedeutic to Christian love and faith, but, given Kierkegaard's parallelism of the public and the private spheres, and given his claim that the public sphere influences the private sphere, certain forms of civic association can serve the same religiously upbuilding function. In some ways natural forms of human social experience can foster virtues that prepare an individual for religious subjectivity.

# 5 The Uniqueness of This Life-View

## What This Life-View Is Not

This way of engaging life, so unusual in Kierkegaard's authorship, is not a variant of the purely aesthetic, ethical, or religious spheres of existence. In this book he distinguished the various life-views according to their respective ways of coping with disappointment, frustration, and anguish. This strategy makes sense given the fact that the novella's plot is structured around the pain of star-crossed romances. Kierkegaard opined that all life-views are, at least in part, responses to suffering. All of them offer a distinctive way of dealing with life's inevitable woes; in Kierkegaard's language, each of them "knows a way out." He wrote, "Every life-view knows the way out [of the pain of actuality], and is cognizable by the way out that it knows" (TA, 15).

According to Kierkegaard, this life-view is not reducible to any form of the aesthetic life. It is certainly not immediate aestheticism, for aestheticism is not self-reflective enough to even know that it needs a "way out" (TA, 20). Moreover, in this life-view an individual is not translated into the ideal realm, as is the case with more sophisticated forms of aestheticism. Poetry, he maintains, does not reconcile the individual with actuality, but only with a projected ideality (TA, 20). He writes, "Esthetically the individual is led away from actuality and translated into the medium of the imagination" (TA, 20). But the life-view enacted in the novella is certainly not imagination's flight to the projected realm of perfection. By saying this, Kierkegaard distinguishes the novella from the sensibilities of the more reflective devotees of Romanticism.

Nor can this life-view be identified with purely ethical existence, although there are some parallels. Kierkegaard wrote pointedly that "the ethical is not decisively contributory" (TA, 40). This life-view as embodied in the main female characters lacks the concern for universal norms and cultural conceptions of duty that characterize ethical life (TA, 40). The two heroines are not transformed and sanctified by the ethical; each one experiences no "ethical deepening of her inner being" (TA, 40). The spiritually salubrious aspects of this life-view, Kierkegaard noted, are not proclaimed by the author authoritatively as if they were categorical ethical precepts that the reader is obligated to adopt and follow.

Moreover, this life-view is clearly not the rigorous striving of the religious life, involving such forms of pathos as resignation, suffering, and guilt. Kierkegaard writes: "But in these stories the author never gets into the kind of pain of actuality that can find its reassurance only in specifically religious categories and in the ideality of the religious" (TA, 15). This was an important point for Kierkegaard, for he explored the contrasts between this author's life-view and a religious life-view in detail. In these stories the author never touches upon the comprehensive discontent with finite existence that can only find solace in the religious life. Although the immediate coherence of immediacy and happiness has been broken in this life-view, as it is in the religious sphere, this rupture does not generate the sweeping despair that can lead to a qualitatively new religious life. Religiously, an individual is translated into the eternal, renouncing aspirations for worldly happiness. However, this life-view is decidedly not a leap away from temporal actuality. Because of the absence of total resignation, it fails to provide the "rest" that religion alone can furnish. Reflecting on the differences between this life-view and religious existence, Kierkegaard remarked that "a person finds definitive rest only in the highest idea, which is the religious" (TA, 65).

Far from being ethical or religious, in some respects this life-view remains firmly within the boundaries of immediacy. It is "immediate" in the sense that the adoption of this way of engaging life is not the product of deliberation and volition. Neither Claudine nor Mariane decides to fall in love, nor do they reflectively choose the objects of their love. Kierkegaard observes that "her [Claudine's] constancy is mainly a natural endowment, a matter of immediacy and romantic erotic love" (TA, 39). Her illicit liaison that produced a child and her continuing fidelity to her beloved are essentially manifestations of the same immediate passion (TA, 45). At least in its origins, this life-view is not a self-conscious, responsible choice of an existential policy. The attraction to the other is more of an urge that happens to a person rather than an intentional act. As such, it is dependent upon such externalities as the initial attractiveness of the beloved, and in this sense has something in common with the aesthetic life. Accordingly, Kierkegaard remarks that falling in love is an unchosen passivity, like being born. Nevertheless, as we shall see, the romantic passion must be intentionally preserved and cultivated.

## What This Life-View Is

*Two Ages'* life-view, Kierkegaard asserted, is "actuality's way out" (TA, 15). It enables individuals to see and appreciate the more healing potentials in their situations and to affirm the goodness of life despite manifold tragedies and disappointments. According to Kierkegaard, the whole series of stories from the author's long career have a "sustaining" impact (TA, 14). Kierkegaard claimed that this life-view supports "the bruised and broken one until he recovers again" (TA, 20). This life-view is a time of healing, in the way that "a bent and bruised flower is held by the stalk until it gets its strength" (TA, 20).

Kierkegaard summarized that this pathos is "resignation's quiet joy over life" (TA, 13). Without being naïve or unrealistic, it hopes that all will be well again. Kierkegaard added that not only does everything get to be good again at the end of the narrative, but that everything has been and remains good, "by using common sense so as to see a more merciful aspect of the suffering, by having the patience that expects good fortune to smile once again, by the friendly sympathy of loving people, by the resignation that gives up – not everything, but the highest – and by the contentment that changes the next best into something just as good as the highest" (TA, 19). Unlike the religious stance, this life-view does not find comfort only in God. Nor does it culminate in an attitude of heart-rending tragedy or nihilistic despair. Its mood is neither the "excited call to battle" nor "the shriek of despair" (TA, 19).

After differentiating this elusive life-view from the religious one, Kierkegaard proceeded to deconstruct any absolute dichotomy of the two. At the very beginning of the review, he lauds this life-view because it "lies on the boundary of the esthetic and in the direction of the religious" (TA, 14). Later he reiterates the claim that this "view is mid-way between the esthetic and the religious" (TA, 39). It is significant that here he omits any reference to a passage through the ethical sphere. He commends it as "a place of rest, or, if you please, a place of prayer, for a certain religious tinge is unmistakable" (TA, 21). Using language typically reserved for religious attitudes, he states that "there is a peace here and the incorruptibility of a quiet spirit" (TA, 16).

According to Kierkegaard, this life-view is not something that a religious individual can ignore. Its virtues should be incorporated into the religious life. He exhorts those looking for decisive religious categories not to discard this life-view, but to continue to honor and appreciate it (TA, 22). Kierkegaard recommends that the religious enthusiast should submit to its guidance and accept its instruction (TA, 13). The religious individual must be reminded to refrain from skipping over the difficulties in life, but to face them with clear-eyed realism (TA, 22). This pedagogy remains necessary even for the zealous individual who "does not rashly hope in the world" and "wants success and failure to signify equally much, that is, equally little" (TA, 13). Even an intensely religious enthusiast could and should learn from the author's faithfulness to herself. Kierkegaard concludes that "there is something to learn here; yes, everyone, whether he is an author or not, can learn something from this, since everyone can learn from the universally paradigmatic, and faithfulness to oneself is the universally paradigmatic" (TA, 13). The intentionally religious individual has not advanced beyond the need for this guidance and instruction, but still needs the reinforcement that the exemplary but not religious lives of the two women can offer (TA, 13).

The communication of this life-view requires a distinctive authorial voice and literary mood. Accordingly, Kierkegaard emphasizes the fact that this author "persuades" (TA, 19). The viability and value of this life-view is not objectively discussed or argued for by the author. For example, the peace with which the story ends is not stated discursively, but is simply shown though the narrative (TA, 19). In the novella quarrels are patched up, displaying the beauty of reconciliation. The attractiveness or necessity of reconciliation is not demonstrated through a Hegelian-style philosophical argument; its beauty is just manifested through the plot and the literary style. The novella's mood is neither analytic nor polemical but is "the inviting intimacy of the cozy inner sanctum" (TA, 19).

This persuasion is compelling not because any new information about life is communicated. Its effectiveness is not a function of an instructive analysis of existence that reveals new truths, nor is it predicated upon a unique revelation. Rather, the novella fosters an accentuated appreciation of the actuality with which everyone is already familiar (TA, 20). The individual is not encouraged to adopt a new ideology, convert to a new religion, or engage in revolutionary change but is persuaded to "remain where one is" (TA, 20). Persuasion, Kierkegaard remarks, "is a movement on the spot," firmly rooted in actuality (TA, 20). The purpose of the novella is to remind a reader of what we all know more or less clearly (TA, 12). Consequently, Kierkegaard can describe this life-view as "common sense mitigated and refined by persuasive feeling and imagination" (TA, 21).

Persuasion demands something of the reader; persuasion is not automatically efficacious through the power of the text. Kierkegaard declares in the preface, "Moreover, it will be readily apparent that this review is not for the esthetic and critical readers of newspapers but for rational creatures who take the time and have the patience to read a little book, although not necessarily this one" (TA, 5). To be persuaded one must listen appropriately. Individuals immersed in pure immediacy cannot listen productively to persuasion because they do not even know that they need healing. Persuasion requires a sense of one's own individuality and particularity, including one's vulnerability. Such self-consciousness can only flourish in a mood of solitude and silence in which the individual is alone with herself, insulated from the distracting noise of the world. In "Purity of Heart Is to Will One Thing," composed about the same time, Kierkegaard writes: "No, busyness – in which one continually goes further and further, and noise in which the true is continually forgotten more and more, and the multitude of circumstances, incentives, and hindrances – continually makes it more impossible for one to gain any deeper knowledge of oneself" (UDVA, 67). Kierkegaard concluded that this self-awareness and sense of self-responsibility is incompatible with obsession about the noisy and ephemeral demands of the times. The insulation of oneself from such distractions can be a crucial practice that is conducive to the growth of inwardness that the religious life requires. In this way, cultivating the proper disposition to read a novella like this one is itself a pedagogy in virtue.

## 6 The Virtues of True Romance

### On the Boundary of the Aesthetic and the Religious

These appreciative remarks about the romances in the novella are very different from Kierkegaard's identification of romance with self-love in portions of *Works of Love*. Far from being the opposite of Christian love for the neighbor, here romantic attachments are situated on the border of the religious life in general and the Christian life in particular. Even more strikingly, romantic attachments of a certain sort can serve as a pedagogy in virtues that are essential for the religious life. Kierkegaard's language suggests that this type of romance, if genuine, can support and encourage dispositions that need to be taken up in the religious life.

The virtues of this attitude toward life are persuasively and sympathetically depicted as attractive existential possibilities, as an "occasion for inwardness" (TA, 16). According to Kierkegaard, the author of the novel serves as a virtuous guide, encouraging the reader to consider these virtues as viable life options, and thereby coaxing the reader toward the very brink of the religious sphere.

## A Qualified Resignation

The relevant dispositions that romance fosters are multiple. Most frequently, Kierkegaard highlights the opportunity to grow in resignation afforded by romance. Gendering the life-view of the novel, he wrote that it portrays an "almost feminine resignation that nevertheless inspires respect" (TA, 16). Kierkegaard insists that the disposition depicted in *Two Ages* is a special sort of qualified renunciation, quite unlike the types that he and his pseudonyms describe elsewhere. It differs markedly from the varieties portrayed in *Fear and Trembling*. It is not the infinite resignation associated with the religious life, for it is not a total break with "actuality," with all the joys, sorrows, hopes, and fears of ordinary earthly life (FT, 38–46). Unlike the infinite type, this resignation does not give up everything, but only the highest hope for earthly happiness (TA, 19). Because it has not given up everything, it cannot have the paradoxical faith that, by virtue of the absurd, everything will be restored. Rather, this life-view hopes for a possible, but improbable, finite resolution.

The dual stories in *Two Ages* involve the concentration of passion and the hope for happiness on a singular beloved object, followed by a tragic obstacle to the relationship's realization. Recognizing the unlikelihood of the satisfaction of the heart's deepest desire, this life-view cultivates a contentment with the next best thing (TA, 19). Even if the relationship is not actually frustrated, a genuine lover knows that the sword of Damocles hangs over the bond and is acutely aware that the thread could always snap. But whether the relationship prospers or is thwarted, Kierkegaard praised this variety of resignation's "quiet joy over life," which is its sense that life can still be tolerably good despite of the disappointment of one's highest hope, or the threat to it (TA, 13). Consequently, the frustration of the highest desire for earthly happiness does not degenerate into a disenchantment with earthly life in general. For example, Kierkegaard remarks that in the novella this resignation involves a willingness to take comfort in the kindness of strangers and in the lesser blessings that providence may provide (TA, 20). Claudine's gratitude to the old housekeeper who rescued her, a virtue that she cultivates, is an example of her capacity to appreciate the beneficent aspects of life (TA, 42). Similarly, Claudine's new baby is an unexpected consolation, making growth in a different love possible.

## Earnestness and Actuality

Kierkegaard describes this life-view as a form of earnestness, a cultivated willingness to embrace tragedy-laden actuality. According to Kierkegaard, this life-view involves an intentional affirmation of actuality despite life's manifold woes. It has a sad familiarity with actuality, but nevertheless expects and appreciates moments of joy (TA, 13). Far from turning away from actuality in bitter disappointment, it finds solace in ordinary things, such as the friendly sympathy of loving people. It remains firmly rooted in the concrete vicissitudes and solaces of earthly life. This life-view rejects the aesthetic flight from concrete existence into the ideal realm of the imagination. It refuses to poeticize its sorrow into art, and thereby trivialize it. Moreover, it does not embrace the more radical consolations of religion's shift of focus to the eternal.

## The Virtue of Patience

This life-view also involves the nurturing of patience, a *sine qua non* for the religious life. It is open to the possibility that good fortune may smile once again (TA, 19). Unlike infinite resignation, the heroines do not renounce all hope for future felicity in this life. The two women continue to imagine the possibility of earthly happiness, fully cognizant of its improbability, without demanding or expecting immediate satisfaction. An eventual reunion with the beloved is not ruled out, and is actively hoped for, even though such a reconciliation is not required for maintaining an affirmative attitude toward life.

## The Virtue of Devotion

Furthermore, this sort of romantic attachment can be a pedagogy in quiet, steadfast devotion. The two heroines cherish the recollection of their lost loves. For example, Claudine remains true to her love despite Lusard's departure to rejoin the French army. For Claudine, treasuring the memory of her beloved is enough to inspire her continuing fidelity. Although Claudine's and Mariane's attachments were originally motivated by an immediate passion, they become a disposition that both women deliberately reinforce and intentionally preserve. Although the perpetuation of their loves continues to be fueled by natural affections, now the preservation of those affections becomes a matter of deliberate and conscious husbandry. Emphasizing this steadfast intentionality to the maximum degree, Kierkegaard asserts that "the spirit" is identical "with resolution in passion" (TA, 22).

## The Meta-Virtue of Inwardness

For Kierkegaard, romantic relationships can be a stimulus for fostering the crucial quality of inwardness which is essential for the authentic selfhood that the religious life presupposes (TA, 16). "Inwardness" in Kierkegaard's pages is a kind of meta-virtue, an overarching disposition informing all aspects of a life and motivating and governing subordinate virtues. Inwardness is the quality of being conscious and mindful of the shape and direction of one's own life, even when the impetus for that life is immediately given and has not been chosen from among alternatives. With inwardness the individual is disposed to assume responsibility for that life, and to feel passionately the momentousness of that responsibility. Kierkegaard insists that in the relationships depicted in *Two Ages* such a genuine inwardness is to be found. Because of this inwardness, he adds that the religious life is not far away (TA, 49). Kierkegaard asserts: "No doubt it is true that the life of being and falling in love is inwardness" (TA, 49) and later links this inwardness with the development of character (TA, 78). For example, he notes that Mariane acquires the "incorruptible nature of a quiet inwardness" amid life's vicissitudes and society's triviality (TA, 48).

This sort of inwardness, Kierkegaard claims, is birthed because romance involves a double existence, as the individual's existential attention is both inwardly and outwardly directed (TA, 49). Kierkegaard claims: "Being in love is the culmination of a person's purely human existence, and for that very reason being in love is simultaneously just as much inwardness as it is a relation directed outwardly to actuality" (TA, 49). Although the ostensible focus is the beloved object, the individual's attention is also riveted on her own subjectivity, for she cares passionately about being worthy of the relationship and labors to sustain the inner fortitude that will enable her feelings about the beloved to endure. The true lover strives to remain true to the idea of the relationship despite obstacles and changing circumstances. This self-cultivation requires the sort of intention and volition characteristic of a classical virtue.

By cultivating this inward concern, the two women remain "true to themselves." Each one had defined herself as a faithful lover; that fidelity had become their identities. Kierkegaard observed that both Claudine and Mariane strove to be faithful to themselves with equal ardor, even though their environments differed greatly. Kierkegaard writes, "Mariane wanted to be true to herself with the same inwardness as Claudine, and yet her love affair would forever be essentially different from Claudine's" (TA, 49).

## The Meta-Virtue of Willing One Thing

Closely related to this growth in inwardness, Kierkegaard maintains, romance provides a pedagogy in "willing one thing." In Kierkegaard's conception of a genuine romantic relationship, the individual loves a particular individual rather than dispersing her desires throughout an expansive field of human beings. The lover is not like a stockbroker who shrewdly diversifies his investments in order to protect himself from financial disappointment. Kierkegaard observed that many of the characters in the novel from the contemporary age fail miserably to will one thing. Some squander their romantic attentions in philandering, which is the negation of the distinction of love and debauchery. Flirting, he claimed, is a kind of anemic and cowardly promiscuity. In the novella the coquettish Mrs. Waller does not will one thing and thereby demonstrates a deplorable lack of character (TA, 53). In opposition to this behavior, the type of romance that the novella porrays favorably consciously preserves the specificity of its focus. The concentration of the passion on one object, including the awareness of the possibility of an unhappy ending, intensifies the lover's concern for the relationship and for life in general. Every romance concentrated on a single beloved involves risk, and risk intensifies passion. The placing of all one's hopes for romantic fulfillment in one basket heightens the awareness of life's uncertainty and fragility. For Kierkegaard, this pedagogy through romance has religious value, for the crucial singularity of its focus and the consequent consciousness of risk is a necessary dimension of all genuine religious subjectivity. A similar approbative attitude to romance is found in *Upbuilding Discourses in Various Spirits*, where Kierkegaard points out: "And certainly it is blissful to be in love: to have only one wish, even if everything else is given or denied – one wish, the beloved – one longing, the beloved – one possession, the beloved," even though this is not the highest willing of the good (UDVS, 109).

## 7 *Two Ages* and the Spheres of the Private and the Public

## The Reflection of the Public in the Private

The appreciation of aspects of romance is not the only noteworthy aspect of Kierkegaard's review of Thomasine Gyllembourg's novella. Equally consequential is the story's foundational supposition that the public sphere is reflected in the private sphere. Kierkegaard notes that the slender volume illustrates this point through its ingenious structure. He repeatedly emphasizes the subtle manifestation of the spirits of the two different ages in interpersonal life. The macro-scale cultural attitudes are reproduced in the micro-scale interpersonal relationships. Kierkegaard writes: "The novel has as its premise the distinctive totality of the age, and the production is the reflection of this in domestic life; the mind turns from the production back again to the totality of the age that has been so clearly revealed in this reflexion" (TA, 32). He affirms that the inwardness can be the same in the two different ages while it manifests itself differently. In fact, the genius of the novel is that it explores how the same life-view can appear in different guises in different cultural contexts (TA, 76). A certain generic virtue, such as loyalty to a beloved, can express itself in very different forms in different eras. For example, in the Middle Ages a romantic girl faced with a doomed romance could have entered a convent as a way of preserving her love in remembrance. But in the age of revolution, she would have been more prone to indulge in an illicit affair with the beloved (TA, 42). This is most evident in the environing culture's decisive impact upon the shape of the romances of the main characters. Kierkegaard summarized this theme by declaring that even falling in love is "greatly influenced by conditions" (TA, 49).

Of course, Kierkegaard was no cultural determinist. He did qualify the influence of the broader cultural sphere on the individual's intimate intersubjective relations. He admits that the characters, both in regard to romantic attachments and political commitments, could appear in any age (TA, 33). Along these lines Kierkegaard remarks that an individual can be a good or a bad person in either generation (TA, 76–77). Nevertheless, Kierkegaard claims, in some eras certain types of characters are more typical and representative because they are encouraged by specific cultural dynamics and social structures (TA, 33).

Further distancing himself from any cultural determinism, Kierkegaard cautions that an age does not have automatic consequences in individual psyches or in social relationships. The issue is not just that cultural contexts differ and shape a life-view differently. Rather, individual psychological characteristics, idiosyncratic motivations, and uncoerced decisions decisively affect the way that the power of the cultural environment operates. Although the development of individual identity is mediated by the "middle-term" of the age, that individuality is not merely a function of the age's spirit (TA, 47). Accordingly, Kierkegaard admires the author's artistry in preventing her characters from being nothing more than one-dimensional examples of the predominant cultural mood.

Kierkegaard suggests that the ethos of an age does much more than inflect the attitudes and dispositions that constitute a life-view. Crucially, he argues that some virtues may be much easier to develop in certain ages than in others. For example, one age may encourage fervent risk-taking, while another may foster prudent analyses of the probable outcomes of actions. By itself, this observation does not necessarily suggest a moral hierarchy of one age over the other. The two virtues, risk-taking and prudence, are very different, but each can contribute relevant qualities to an earnest life. An earnest life requires both passion and courage on the one hand and an honest assessment of the costs of a responsible life on the other. In spite of this, it is possible that the sensibilities of a particular age might encourage some virtues that are more important than others or might be more susceptible to certain vices that are more pernicious than others. It is also possible that an age might be uniquely ill-suited to the fostering of any religiously significant virtues.

## The Differences among the Virtues of the Two Ages

Kierkegaard's accentuation of the differences between the two ages implies that the romantic virtues encouraged by natural forms of sociability will differ at least somewhat from culture to culture and epoch to epoch. In spite of the important commonalities informing the life-view of the two romances, there are differences between the virtues of the two heroines due to the differences between their two different historical or cultural contexts. The novel, he enthuses, dramatizes these differences admirably through the interaction of context, character, and events (TA, 32).

## Passion and Reflection

Kierkegaard's assessment of the different potencies of the age of revolution and the present age concentrate mostly upon the difference between passion and reflection. In Kierkegaard's view the author's portrayal of the revolutionary age uncovers the failings of the contemporary age by providing a clear contrast. Much of his review is an exposé of the "fruitlessness of reflection" and the need for a recovery of passion (TA, 66). For Kierkegaard, "reflection" in this context suggests a calculating prudence; it is indecisive toying with possibilities rather than passionate decisiveness. The author, he concludes, presents the revolutionary age as an era of passionate political and ethical idealism, while the contemporary age is a time of prosaic, prudential reflection, devoid of passion. Kierkegaard says, "life in the present age is not disturbed by that energetic passion that has its form in its very energy. . . . On the contrary, everything is manifestly nondescript, thus trivial, formless, superficial, obsequious, and openly so" (TA, 29). As a result, cultural life devolves into an inchoate mush in which everything is just about equally important. In his journals he repeats this diagnosis, writing: "What our times need is pathos" (KJN 4, 119).

The passionate ethos of the revolutionary age had formed characters who possessed the virtues of decisiveness and boldness. For example, Kierkegaard describes Lusard as being excitable in all his moods; his romantic ardor is reflected in his political zeal. Kierkegaard applauds this type of bold action "even if it is a rash leap, if only it is decisive" (TA, 71). This risk-taking disposition would help a person to become an individual. In contrast to this, the prudential present age discourages the making of decisions. Reflection indulges in the endless projection of possibilities and the weighing of possible outcomes, making closure impossible. Kierkegaard writes that reflection is so tempting "because one single clever fabrication is able to give the matter a sudden new turn, because reflection is able at any moment to reinterpret, and allow one to escape somewhere, because even in the final moment of reflective decision it is possible to do it all over again" (TA, 77). The tendency of the present age is to be paralyzed by irresolution and clever equivocations (TA, 69). But, try as it might, the present age has not succeeded in nullifying the principle of contradiction, for life demands that individuals are obliged to make a choice among alternative courses of action (TA, 66–67, 97). Kierkegaard takes comfort in the fact that the existential "either/or" is still in force.

Although Kierkegaard often described Claudine more favorably, he portrayed each of the female characters as possessing virtues that have potential religious value. Most importantly, Claudine is described as being impulsive while Mariane is more reflective and cautious (TA, 42–45). In Kierkegaard's eyes Claudine's willingness to take risks is laudable, even though it does result in "a lapse from virtue" (TA, 45). Her passionate daring could accustom her to taking the kind of leap amid uncertainty that faith requires. As a consequence, Claudine matures in inwardness due to the recklessness of her singular romantic attachment.

But, according to Kierkegaard, Mariane's reflection is also an asset. Mariane learns early in her life to practice "the incorruptible nature of a quiet inwardness" (TA, 48). Having grown up in an unsupportive and cautious household, she does not expect the world to indulge her hopes and desires. By the time that she reaches adulthood she is already accustomed to renunciation (TA, 49–50). Mariane's inwardness is characterized by the "quiet virtues" of a maiden who accepts the reality that her fidelity to her love will involve suffering (TA, 51). Mariane's sober evaluation of the discouraging social context of her romance prompts further resignation, and therefore further inwardness. Although her habitual resignation is largely the product of environmental factors, in this romance it becomes something that she intentionally accepts and endorses. Her cultivated resignation and realism can become virtues that would be essential for the blossoming of faith.

Both dispositions also possess liabilities. Claudine's risk-taking can devolve into a rashness that is not mature courage. Her assessments of the obstacles in the social world and their consequences for her life are naïve. Consequently, her actions are sometimes intemperate, as is the case with her pregnancy. In an opposite manner, Mariane's reflectiveness (and her lover Bergland's hesitations) can lead to paralyzing indecision (TA 52–53). Kierkegaard sometimes hints that Mariane's sensibility is more problematic than Claudine's, for the age of reflection has made it difficult for her to develop the courage to risk everything by taking decisive action (TA, 50). It is easier for a passionate individual to learn to be prudent than it is for a reflective person to learn to be bold.

But in spite of these differences, Kierkegaard insists that the novella practices a strict impartiality in regard to the relative value of the two ages. He protests: "Incidentally, the question of which age is the better one, the more significant, does not enter into the novel itself (a model, I must say), or into this review, imitating the novel, subordinate to it, and in its service" (TA, 76). Kierkegaard praises the author for having resisted the temptation to evaluate the spirits of the two ages and for restricting herself to the task of comparing them.

To support his assessment of the author's impartiality, Kierkegaard remarks that even if she seems to prefer the revolutionary age's soul-stirring vitality, this is balanced by her greater artistry in describing the present age (TA, 34). In the depiction of the present age the characters stand out in exquisite particularity, while in the portrayal of the revolutionary age their more idiosyncratic features are obscured by the intensity of their passion (TA, 35). The revolutionary characters stand out less clearly as unique and complex individuals precisely because they exist in a state of passion. The focus on the overwhelming power of the revolutionary passion would have made attention to externalities a distraction. In contrast, Kierkegaard added that the author's account of the present age is graced with vivid descriptions of the cultural context and psychological details, although most of the depicted characters exhibit dull triviality. According to Kierkegaard, this is appropriate, for the personalities of the present age possess no inner dynamics to draw attention away from contextual details (TA 35–36). In spite of the ostensible preference for the passionate age of revolution, attention to both inner passion and outer circumstances are potentially valuable dispositions for the religious life. These remarks about the differing literary strategies in depicting the two ages enabled Kierkegaard to argue that the same distinctive life-view is present in both ages, while still maintaining that the culture of an age inflects the life-view differently, producing different religiously valuable virtues.

Kierkegaard suggests that the ideal would be for the virtues exemplified by the two women to be combined into a reflective passion. Reflection is not bad in itself; it is higher than immediacy because it involves greater self-awareness and more considered intention. He writes, "Reflection is not the evil, but the state of reflection, stagnation in reflection, is the abuse and the corruption that occasion retrogression by transforming the perquisites into evasions" (TA, 96). In fact, Kierkegaard opined that in the present age an immediate enthusiast would not help bring about cultural remediation (KJN 4, 119). Revitalization will not take the form of a direct return to the passionate ethos of the revolutionary age. Such a return is neither possible or nor desirable. Rather, individuals do need to be reflective, but they must imbue their reflection with decisiveness and passion. Because the present age is more reflectively developed, it could act more intensively, with all its actions informed by deliberation and cognizance of probable consequences (TA, 110). True action, he contends, goes hand in hand with circumspection. Kierkegaard concludes approvingly that the author has found such beneficial elements in both ages.

Kierkegaard sometimes proposes that robust, genuine action requires first a period of immediate, spontaneous inspiration, then a period of reflective prudence, and finally a period of the highest enthusiasm that perceives what the prudent thing to do would be, but rejects it and thereby experiences infinite enthusiasm. For example, Socrates was not rash, but perceived what prudence would dictate, and then rejected it in order to remain true to himself (TA, 111). The highest form of inwardness is capable of acting against the prudential understanding. Because of this, the virtues of both ages can be equally legitimate, and their synthesis in a reflective passion that accepts self-sacrifice would be optimal (TA, 110).

To conclude, through this discussion of the two heroines Kierkegaard has proposed that a certain type of romance, appropriated in an intentional way, can foster many of the dispositions, attitudes, and virtues that are crucial for the religious life. Most prominently, these include constancy, resignation, singularity of focus, patience, steadfastness, and the appreciation of life's minor blessings. All of these are associated with the meta-disposition of inwardness. Inwardness and these subsidiary dispositions are the very qualities that loom large in Kierkegaard's upbuilding and Christian discourses, some of which he had defined before writing the review. For example, Kierkegaard's valorization of the expectant patience of the New Testament character Anna employs the same language to describe her character that he uses to describe the patience of Claudine and Mariane (EUD, 209–218). Similarly, Kierkegaard's myriad exhortations in the upbuilding discourses to look for joy in the midst of suffering are reminiscent of the attitude of Claudine and Mariane. It might not be too fanciful to suggest that for Kierkegaard these virtues were cardinal, in Aquinas's sense, because the theological virtues associated with love for God and neighbor presuppose them.

## 8 The Formative Power of Cultural and Political Life

### The Pedagogy of Civil Associations

The parallelism of the two romances and the political ethoi of the two different ages suggest a bolder and potentially more controversial claim. It is significant that Kierkegaard's appreciation of the novel hinges not only on its enactment of a distinctive and attractive life-view, but also on the hints in the text that the virtues developed in interpersonal relationships have counterparts in broader public forms of association. Kierkegaard insists throughout his review that the public domain shapes and colors the manifestation of romance in the interpersonal realm, often in ways that are positive. This could not happen if the virtues encouraged by romance were totally incongruous with at least some of the dispositions encouraged by certain forms of civic association. By implication, just as the virtues associated with genuine romance can serve as a pedagogy for religious virtues, so also can the virtues associated with certain forms of civic life serve as a similarly upbuilding education. Of course, forms of civic life can also foster vices that are inimical to religious life, and Kierkegaard does spend most of his time in the latter half of the book exposing the vices of the present age.

## The Political Context of *Two Ages*

Kierkegaard's fragmentary remarks about civic associations must be situated in his historical context, for his comments were, in part, responses to the dynamics in his cultural and political environment. An "enlightened" absolutist regime with a powerful monarchial bureaucracy had ruled Denmark from 1660.[36] The absolute monarchy was supported by mercantile, professional, and bureaucratic elites that benefited from its patronage. By the end of the eighteenth-century, shipping was no longer the dynamo that it had been, a decline exacerbated by the Napoleonic wars, and the economy began to rely more on agriculture. The traditional system of large landowners renting out farmland in a haphazard manner was increasingly seen as being inefficient by the royal advisors. Their attempted reforms benefited the middling landowners, but not the landless "cottagers." Impersonal market forces rather than personal relations with landlords and fellow villagers disrupted village life. Socialism began to make some headway in the population, as the downturn accentuated class distinctions and alarmed many of the Golden Age elites.

In 1838 the progressive activist Orla Lehmann (1810–1870) championed the landless peasants' calls for further reform and forged a new alliance of urban liberals and peasants. This alliance inspired the mass meetings of 1846 that institutionalized the reform movement, including its calls for further land reform and the extension of the franchise. This populist movement was in full swing as Kierkegaard was composing *Two Ages: A Literary Review*. His journals show that he was well aware of the discontent and could view the crowds gathering in the streets from his window.

Other factors contributed to the political uncertainty. The upper-middle class liberals, ardent about free trade and reduced royal expenditure, agitated for lower tariffs and protested the stringent censorship that King Frederick had enacted. Meanwhile, more radical writers like M. A. Goldschmidt (1819–1887) and activists like Lehmann began to demand universal male suffrage. (Goldschmidt was the editor of the scurrilous periodical *The Corsair* that lampooned Kierkegaard about the same time that he was composing his literary

---

[36] See Bruce H. Kirmmse, *Kierkegaard in Golden Age Denmark* (Bloomington: Indiana University Press, 1990), 9–25.

review.) By the 1840's the liberal reform movement had solidified and calls for a constitution became more strident. When Christian VIII died in 1848 and was succeeded by Frederick VII, the liberals would gain momentum and the old regime would be supplanted by a constitutional monarchy in which actual power was vested in a representative assembly. Kierkegaard's journals show that he closely followed these various calls for reform and the reaction against them.

To further destabilize the political situation, the question of the relation of the Danish nation to the two southern Jutland regions of Schleswig and Holstein became acute. Holstein, a personal possession of the crown, was not a part of the Danish state but was a member of the German Confederation. Half of the population of Schleswig, which enjoyed a high degree of regional autonomy, was German-speaking. With the ominous rise of Prussia, many Danes feared that the two regions would become German territory and demanded that they be organically integrated into the Danish state. By 1846 even the younger generation of liberals led by Lehmann, energized by Nordic jingoism, urged the government to come to the aid of the Danish-speaking population in southern Jutland.

Fears of chaotic populism motivated the old haute bourgeoisie of Copenhagen, including the clergy and the literary establishment, to champion absolutism and resist the movements for the enlargement of the electorate. Even the old moderate liberals like H. N. Clausen, Kierkegaard's former theology professor, insisted that participation in political decisions required education in humane culture and should not be the privilege of unschooled common people. This lionization of elite culture was a characteristic of the Golden Age social circles in which Kierkegaard had been raised.

To an extent Kierkegaard shared the cultural elite's disdain for the materialism of the commercial classes. In 1847 he mourned, "No, here in this country anyone working disinterestedly for an idea but without a living loses all respect – for to pursue, to acquire, to live lazily in a living, that is good morals – the alternative is immorality" (KJN 4, 253). In a journal entry from 1847 or early 1848 he complained that twenty years of peace had led to a spiritually stifling prosperity and "a brash worldliness" (KJN 4, 302).

Bishop Jacob Peter Mynster (1775–1854) and his successor Bishop Martensen, the arbiters of "Golden Age" religious culture, were apprehensive about the burgeoning of lay democracy, fearing that church doctrines and policies would be controlled by fickle popular opinion. Mynster tended to conflate Christianity with "cultivation," the internalization of the traditions, values, and tastes of the educated class. Similarly, in his *Outline of Moral Philosophy*, a book which Kierkegaard owned, Martensen contended that the blossoming of the Christian nation was essential for the faith and for human civility.[37] Later Martensen would write that the divine/human spirit had been progressively actualized in the Lutheran nation-state, which had created political and cultural structures that nurture Christian faith.[38] Although Martensen distinguished the state from God's kingdom as such, the support of the state was essential for the suffusion of the church's values into all the dimensions of the cultural world that shape the individual. The individual could not pursue reconciliation with God without being immersed in an appropriately God-oriented Christian culture. For ecclesiasts like Martensen, the institutions and dynamics of the nation mediate the relationship of God and the individual.

The state church was incarnated in certain institutional structures, most of which were being challenged. Until 1849 the Evangelical Lutheran State Church of Denmark was indirectly managed by the royal administration and lacked any formal constitution of its own. By 1846 a movement was gaining strength to create a "People's Church" under the direct rule of the hoped-for new constitutional government. Ostensibly the ecclesial institutions would not be changed, but the church would become an agency of the electorate. While he was writing his literary review, Kierkegaard expressed his fear of this outcome that loomed on the horizon.

Other factions in the church construed its relation to the state differently, although they too fervently supported the symbiosis of Christianity and culture. In his younger days the enormously popular pastor N. F. S. Grundtvig (1783–1872) had recoiled from rationalistic theology and, as an antidote, promoted a close identification of romantic panentheism, nature mysticism, Norse mythology, and Christianity.[39] Although by the 1830's Grundtvig was elevating the spirit of Christianity above natural religiosity, demoting Norse myths to the status of supplemental or preparatory revelations, he did continue to insist that the culture of Denmark, including its political ethos and institutions, were vital for Christianity because people are intrinsically communal beings and develop their moral and spiritual lives collectively. Consequently, Grundtvig concluded that immersion in the political order is a necessary prerequisite for Christian growth. Moreover, he proclaimed that Scandinavia in general and Denmark in particular have a unique role to play in God's plan. The Norse spirit weans people away from the crude materialism and worldly triviality of the

---

[37] Hans Lassen Martensen, *Outline to a System of Moral Philosophy*, in *Between Hegel and Kierkegaard*, trans. by Curtis L. Thompson and David J. Kangas (Atlanta, GA: Scholars Press, 1997), 299.

[38] Hans Lassen Martensen, *Outline to a System of Moral Philosophy*, in *Between Hegel and Kierkegaard*, trans. by Curtis L. Thompson and David J. Kangas (Atlanta, GA: Scholars Press, 1997), 299.

[39] See Nikolaj F. S. Grundtvig, *The Human Comes First: The Christian Theology of N. S. F. Grundtvig*, ed. and trans. Edward Broadbridge (Aarhus: Aarhus University Press, 2018), 55–230.

bourgeoisie and habituates them to the pursuit of values that are more pro-foundly spiritual and communal. In his mature period Grundtvig saw the spiritual revitalization of Denmark as flowing from popular culture and a free marketplace of theological ideas rather than from an absolutist state church.

## Kierkegaard's Explicit Responses to the Political/Cultural Situation

Kierkegaard's written responses to these ecclesial and political controversies that boiled up around 1846 are scattered, impressionistic, and do not fit neatly into any ideological camp. Although Kierkegaard was certainly not interested in formulating a political theory, he was not indifferent to reflection upon politics. His attitude to the state was fluid, evolving, context-dependent, and often ambivalent. Nevertheless, his pointed passing remarks reveal his intense concern about these matters.

Kierkegaard expressed various discontents with all the parties. In 1847 he complained that Mynster talked glowingly about the virtues of a state church and a Christian country while he admitted that only a few people in the country were actually trying to be Christian (KJN 4, 237). In January of 1847, he even accused Mynster of deifying the existing order and confusing the faith with bourgeois philistinism (KJN 4, 81). Also in 1847, Kierkegaard rejected the ethnically inflected nationalism of Grundtvig, declaring it to be nonsense and a regression to the paganism's deification of nationalism (KJN 4, 191). He objected that it is simply not the case that one cannot be a Christian without nationality. He ridiculed Grundtvig's posturing as a prophet of Denmark's superior culture and his advocacy of its claim to be a great nation (KJN 4, 209). In 1848 he dismissed all "the noise about Holstein" as a mere nothing that only served to get "the blood racing for patriotism" (KJN 4, 349).

Kierkegaard's casual remarks often support the accusation of political indifferentism that some expositors have leveled at him. Many of these seemingly apolitical statements were written after he had finished *Two Ages* but before he launched his more strident "attack upon Christendom." Sometime in 1847 or early 1848 Kierkegaard confessed in a letter that "politics is not for me" (LD, 253). In 1848, rather than encouraging structural political and economic change, Kierkegaard asserted that society should "Let him [the worker] do his work and rejoice in it" (PC, 67). In 1850, years after writing the review of *Two Ages*, he asserted explicitly, "Christianity is indifferent to every arrangement of the state, can live equally well under all of them" (KJN 8, 136.) In 1851 in an open letter to Andreas Rudelbach, a pastor who had called for the reformation of the church through political means, Kierkegaard protested that he had never advocated for external institutional change but had only tried to provoke the inward transformation of the individual (COR, 51–60). And in 1851 he repeated the same claim in *Practice in Christianity* (PC, 301).

Sometimes Kierkegaard implied that Christians should be politically indifferent because their focus should be directed to religious matters that are loftier than the material conditions of life. In *Upbuilding Discourses in Various Spirits*, published a year after the literary review, he exhorted Christians to renounce concern for temporal goods in order to focus on eternity (UDVS, 62). According to Kierkegaard, the individual cannot serve God and the world; such an effort would be an exercise in double-mindedness (UDVS, 36). The individual must repress all temporal attachments in order to allow herself to be "healed by the eternal" (UDVS, 113). Only when social ties are relativized can the path to the divine be cleared. When the Schleswig-Holstein war broke out, Kierkegaard complained that the discussion of the war in contemporary sermons got people's attention, but the mention of "God" did not interest them (KJN, 11, p. 2, 185). Similarly, in 1848 he complained, "And during all this commotion [the Schleswig-Holstein war], not a word is heard about religiosity – not a single word. ... Do any of those who now go off to war think about settling their accounts with God [?]" (KJN 4, 350).

Even in 1846 Kierkegaard sometimes advanced beyond indifferentism to outright hostility to political movements and institutions. In the review of *Two Ages* Kierkegaard stridently warned his Danish compatriots about the dangers of identification with all collectivities (TA, 106). Often he seems to have been critical of any form of civic community, even declaring the principle of association in general to be depraved. He lamented that sociality is inherently demoralizing, for in the contemporary age the principle of association is negative, not positive (TA, 106).

Looking beyond the immediate period following the composition of *Two Ages*, Kierkegaard's dissatisfaction with "associations" became more intense. In the journals and papers of 1854, he accentuated the incompatibility of religious inwardness and collectivities, saying, "Now I see what a dreadful distance there is between society and [Christianity]" (KJN 9, 300). Kierkegaard even went so far as to declare that the confusion of Christianity and politics was a symptom of the deeper confusion of Christianity and human nature (SKS 20, 253). In 1854, with Grundtvig in mind, he minimized the pedagogical significance of political community by proclaiming that Christianity does not require that the individual "remain in civil society in order to be morally ennobled" (KJN 10, 280). This sentiment erupted publicly in the radical polemics of his notorious attack upon Christendom of 1854–1855.

Sometimes, especially around 1846, Kierkegaard did qualify his indifferentism and hostility by voicing somewhat anemic endorsements of the monarchy and defenses of traditionalism. He praised the novel because it exhibited no impatience for something new, but expressed an appreciation of the elders (TA, 112). Expressing his conservative proclivities, he cautioned that one should uphold a less than satisfactory established order rather than reforming it too early (KJN 6, 151).

As has often been noted, Kierkegaard's political instincts were basically royalist. Recently Matías Tapia Wende has argued that Kierkegaard remained a champion of the absolutist monarchial state until it proved to be incapable of preserving a social space for authentic Christianity to flourish, or, even worse, until it attempted to interfere with the faith.[40] Indeed, in *Concluding Unscientific Postscript*, during the year before Kierkegaard wrote the literary review, the pseudonym Johannes Climacus exclaims:

> Praise be to the well-ordered state! Enviable happiness be to him who understands how to esteem it! How can anyone be so busy wanting to reform the state and have the form of government changed! Of all forms of government, the monarchical is the best. More than any other form of government, it encourages and protects the secret fancies and innocent foibles of private persons. (CUP I, 620)

Most importantly for Kierkegaard, monarchy allows individuals to focus on matters of existential seriousness rather than on the externalities of politics. By assuming responsibility for governance, the monarchy created a cultural space for individuals to develop their own subjectivities without unnecessary distractions. Kierkegaard lost patience with the traditional order only when he concluded that the very meaning of Christianity was being jeopardized, and only attacked it when he surmised that the political institutions could not be rehabilitated.

The obverse side of Kierkegaard's qualified fondness for monarchy was his distrust of the rationalizing programs of the liberal reformers. He disdained the effort to solve human problems through social engineering and the use of technical reasoning to design more efficient and beneficial political structures. Abstract rationality, he feared, was being given precedence over concrete local cultures and traditions (KJN 2, 275). This reductive and mechanical approach to public issues prioritized formal structures and quantitative calculations over interpersonal relations (TA, 107–108). He feared that this technological strategy, championed by the physiocrats, was backward, for the concrete cultural "idea" should determine the form, not the other way around. Life, he insisted, is not abstract and quantifiable, as the rationalistic bureaucrats assumed, but is highly concrete.

---

[40] Matías Tapia Wende, "The Concept of State in Kierkegaard's *Papers,*" *Kierkegaard Studies Yearbook* 26 (2021): 105–136.

Kierkegaard's predilection for monarchy was also matched by his disdain for populist movements. In 1847 Kierkegaard opined that of all forms of government it is democracy, not monarchy, that is the most potentially despotic (KJN 11, pt. 2, 185). Consequently, contemporary reforming movements should be directed against the "crowd," not the government (KJN 4, 135). Any "people's government," he warned, is devoid of spirit (KJN 11.2, 185). In 1848 he condemned the deification of the masses perpetrated by the opposition to the king (KJN 4, 314). Under a democratic system the functional ruler is the unstable majority of the moment. An individual human being ruling as a tyrant can possess the self-restraint to leave the private sphere alone, but a ruling majority cannot be so benign, for it must actively pander to popular prejudices. Accordingly, in 1848 Kierkegaard cautioned that truly progressive movements will not emerge from "the rumblings of the people" (KJN 4, 340). Continuing this critique, in 1851 he complained that now people want to govern and bully the government (KJN 8, 165).

Most importantly, Kierkegaard feared the subordination of Christianity to fickle popular opinion and the resultant democratization of truth. In 1848 he warned that matters of religion cannot be decided by voting. In any system of voting, truth is determined by majority opinion; it is only the large numbers that count (KJN 4, 372). But, he proclaims, from a Christian perspective, the truth is always in the minority, for the Christian message of self-giving is always offensive to prevalent conceptions of well-being (KJN 4, 372). Voting, he warned, is the divinization of worldliness and self-interest (KJN 4, 371). Kierkegaard lamented that contemporary Danes desiring to participate in a people's government do not really care about fidelity to God (KJN 11.2, 186). He warned that both Christianity and the state would be made impossible by the propagandistic press that fostered a mindless conformism to a mutable and vague "public opinion" (KJN 7, 184).

But Kierkegaard did not remain a consistent monarchist or a defender of traditional hierarchies. At least by 1848 he had become just as condemnatory of the hierarchical church/state establishment as he was of the progressive populist movements. His last writings were addressed to the "common man" and called for a protest against the "establishment," which included the state as well as the church.[41] Throughout his career Kierkegaard railed against the temptation to deify the state, including the monarchial state (KJN 4, 81).

Kierkegaard was neither a thoroughgoing populist nor an ardent counter-revolutionary. He was not even a consistent indifferentist. On the one hand, Kierkegaard feared that the agitation for popular sovereignty generated

---

[41]  See Bukdahl.

adoration of the numerical majority, the reduction of individuals to abstract equality, ephemeral reformist enthusiasms, superficial bonds based on self-interest, affectation, the leveling of distinctions, and envy of other individuals and social groups. The populist authoritarianism, grudgingly tolerated by the weakened old regime, would generate a communalism so powerful that the individuating aspirations of Christianity would be fatally impeded. In Kierkegaard's eyes the old urban liberals were no better, for they merely patronized the common people, even though they secretly despised the commoners' lack of high culture. That condescension was the liberal elite's indulgence in the vices of smugness and deception. On the other hand, he fretted that the conservatives valorized organic bonds of culture and race, equated an individual's identity with her role in a hierarchical system, made religion a tool of social solidarity, and domesticated the church. For Kierkegaard, any sort of automatic conformism to prevalent social or political mores, no matter what their ideological flavor might be, is lethal to the development of the passion necessary for genuine selfhood.

## A Virtue-nurturing Political Culture

In spite of Kierkegaard's evident ambivalence or outright aversion to all the prevalent political movements of his era, in *Two Ages* he did gesture toward the possibility that certain political arrangements and dynamics could serve as a preparation for the virtues that religious existence requires. His cautious and qualified appreciation of certain political movements is evident in his sensitivity to the positive formative power of the age of revolution, especially its impact on the more private domain of romance. The beneficial aspects of that form of romance suggest that there was something positive about the political culture that shaped Claudine, and, in a less obvious way, something similar could be said about the culture that shaped Mariane.

This positive parallelism and interaction between romance and political associations may be clearest in Kierkegaard's description of the virtues characteristic of the age of revolution, as evidenced in the French legation. As Kierkegaard noted, in the novella the ethos of the revolutionary age is represented by "a little band of exceptionally cultured Frenchmen" (TA, 62). The legation is, unashamedly, an ideological faction and a political task force. It is animated by the ideals of the French Revolution, fueled by the values of liberty, equality, and fraternity. One might expect Kierkegaard to excoriate this sort of movement as an example of the spirit-squelching herd mentality and as a paradigmatic instantiation of the nefarious crowd. However, he did not do so.

# 9 The Virtues of the Age of Revolution

## The Passion of the Revolutionary Age

Kierkegaard clearly preferred the age of revolution to the age of reflection, even though he had argued that the life-view of *Two Ages* could occur in either cultural era and that neither the author nor the reviewer intended to adjudicate the relative merits of the two ages. As we have seen, for Kierkegaard the most important thing about the age of revolution was that it possessed passion and therefore had immediacy (TA, 65). With overt admiration Kierkegaard commended the singular ethos of the French legation that instantiated that quality (TA, 25–31, 61–68). Its emotions, thoughts, and actions were heartfelt, sincere, and deep-rooted, springing forth from settled convictions and valuations held with earnestness (TA, 65). All the main characters associated with the embassy are said to have been in a state of intentionally guarded and nurtured passion. Kierkegaard clarified that this is not the first immediacy, in which an individual's feelings and intentions are mere reactions to external phenomena. Moreover, it is not the final immediacy of faith, in which an individual's subjectivity is utterly independent of external circumstances. Unlike faith, to some extent this immediacy still responds to events. Kierkegaard described it as a restoring of natural relations in reaction to fossilized formalism, narrow-hearted custom, and mechanical practice. Although the enthusiasm for an ideal does well up in the self, this passion becomes a virtue as it is intentionally affirmed, cultivated, and preserved. For Kierkegaard, this is admirable, for deliberately engaging life with passion is a premier quality in the self and is a prerequisite for the religious life. This approbative attitude implies that certain political projects, at least of this revolutionary sort, can encourage some virtues that are relevant to the religious life.

Kierkegaard was not so much concerned about the political content of the specific ideals as he was about the way in which they were engaged and internalized by individuals. For example, he had little to say about the ideological content of the convictions of the French legation. Similarly, Kierkegaard observed that the Waller home in Copenhagen in which much of the drama unfolds contained both monarchists and republicans, while he declined to endorse either faction (TA, 25). What interested him was the fact that their political disputes revealed commendable passions on all sides.

Of course, when Kierkegaard praised the passions of the revolutionary age he was not valorizing the violence of the Jacobins. He was far from being an apologist for the Reign of Terror. He remarked that this sociability "is not the dithyrambic songs of revolt that attract crowds" (TA, 63). Rather, he admired the idealism of the reform-minded French constitutionalists. According to Kierkegaard, the members of French legation were not fanatics condemning their enemies to the guillotine. No mob mentality inflamed by collective rage could be found in the French diplomats or in the members of the Waller household.

## Form and Culture

Far from being a chaos of primitive emotional reactions, the passion of the revolutionary age had "form" (TA, 61). According to Kierkegaard, their passion was teleological, aiming at the actualization of ideals. The pursuit of those ideals required the subordination of personal proclivities, whims, and desires to the envisioned goal. Because it was life-shaping, this passion was not like a sober book cover that hides a text of superficial and fleeting emotions. In Kierkegaard's terminology, this passion had "culture" (TA, 61). He asserts that a peasant in love has culture, as does the little band of Frenchmen (TA, 62). Moreover, because this passion generates long-term patterns of publicly observable action, its enactment is a "revelation" of its internal energy and constancy (TA, 66).

## The Virtue of Single-Mindedness

Just as Kierkegaard discerned the virtue of single-mindedness in genuine romance, so also he praised single-minded devotion to a "specific endeavor" (UDVS, 35). Presumably such a focused endeavor would include the political project of the French legation. Shortly after publishing his literary review, he wrote:

> Perhaps there was someone whom enthusiasm gripped for a specific endeavor. Full of enthusiasm, he willed only one thing; he would live and die for this endeavor, he would sacrifice everything for it, in it alone he would have his happiness – because erotic love and enthusiasm are not content with a divided heart. Yet his endeavor may still not have been in the deepest sense the good; thus enthusiasm became for him the teacher he presumably outgrew but to whom he also owed very much. (UDVS, 35)

Kierkegaard's language here echoes almost exactly the words he used in the same upbuilding discourse to applaud the pedagogical potential of single-minded romance.

## Intentionality and Responsibility

In addition to being a paragon of passion and single-mindedness, the French legation exemplified a praiseworthy intentionality and responsibility. Although its members were passionate, their passion was not the effluvia of unreflective sociality. Kierkegaard remarked that individuals who truly embody the revolutionary age were related to one another through an idea (TA, 62). In fact, the original attractiveness of Lusard to Claudine was based on his ability to give her an idea, namely, the values of the French Revolution. According to Kierkegaard, each member of the legation had individually chosen to follow this idea (TA, 62). Their commitment to the revolutionary ideals was voluntary; their community was not the fruit of an immediate social instinct. He observes that this association "is not even the gay and lively songs of conviviality that unites friends" (TA, 63). In his journals from 1847 Kierkegaard criticized assemblies that are nothing more than the sociability of clinking glasses and drinking songs (KJN, 4, 235). A passionate community is not defined by the conviviality of pals. Kierkegaard notes approbatively that the individuals in the French legation "never come too close to one another in the herd sense," but maintained a modest and decent distance (TA, 62). Their bond was the jointly accepted set of political values, not any ties of blood and soil. Their sociality sprang from a source internal to each individual; it was not the product of influential external factors. According to Kierkegaard, the Frenchmen were united to one other only because of the shared idea, to which they were individually and passionately related. Of course, if political partisans were to relate to one another merely on the basis of shared heredity or culture the result would indeed be "crudeness" (TA, 63). Even if individuals relate to a genuine idea, if they adopt it only because others do, vulgar enmeshment would be the result. Communally induced political fervor, like that which is produced by mass meetings, is not genuine community. Kierkegaard was delighted that the sociality of the French legation was not that sort of crudeness (TA, 62). He concludes approvingly that voluntary but shared devotion is the source of genuine "propriety" (TA, 64).

According to Kierkegaard, this mode of social relationality is optimal and normative for political communities. He even enthused that it has a sense of the sacred about it. Echoing a theme from *Concluding Unscientific Postscript*, he likened these political partisans to the pagan idolater who passionately worshiped an objectively false god with subjectively commendable humility. Kierkegaard claims, "when passion is essentially present in the pagan, even his idolatry is not devoid of devoutness; although he has a false concept, he has the idea that one should fear God" (TA, 64).

## Self-Sacrifice

Kierkegaard adds that the age of revolution included yet another virtue: the willingness to make sacrifices for a noble principle. The champions of the revolutionary age, including the French legation, had transcended narrow egoism and the superficialities of the social world. They valued something beyond their own temporal well-being or even the flourishing of their nationality or social class. They had an ideal to live and die for, an ideal that gave their lives direction, cohesion, and purpose. Stressing the importance of self-giving in his journals from 1847, Kierkegaard remarked that genuine "authority" is not a function of an office but of the willingness to sacrifice everything for one's cause (KJN 4, 253). Sadly, he feared that such self-denial was not exhibited by contemporary youth (TA, 71).

## Self-Discipline and Self-Direction

Far from being "free and easy," the age of revolution was "disciplined," a virtue that is associated with Kierkegaard's claim that there "is something sacred" about it (TA, 64). Kierkegaard's use of the word "sacred" here is significant, reflecting what he had said about the nearness of the life-view to the religious sphere. The word "sacred" draws attention to the fact that the crucial qualities of critical self-reflection, self-evaluation, and responsible volition that characterize the religious sphere were also evident in the members of the French legation. Such practice in self-discipline is an invaluable preparation for the religious life.

Closely related to this is another virtue: the self-direction that is a component of inwardness. The revolutionary individuals refused to submit automatically to fossilized social or political formulae (TA, 65). The members of the legation were not reflexively subservient to desiccated customs and traditional practices. Kierkegaard enthused that this bold willingness to step outside the boundaries of inherited cultural and political norms generates "essential inwardness" (TA, 62). Each individual must decide to take that post-conventional leap for himself, without delegating ethical responsibility to any authoritative social group or political party. That inward assumption of responsibility and risk was evident in the political experimentation of the revolutionary zealots, just as much as it was in Claudine's pregnancy out of wedlock. The cultivation of passion fosters courage to contravene the dictates of respectability as defined by the crowd.

## Decisiveness

Furthermore, revolutionary parties can encourage the virtues of decisiveness and concrete action (TA, 66–67). In the French legation, individuals voluntarily took risks, not knowing what the outcome would be. Revolutionaries are not paralyzed by deliberations, as are the denizens of the age of reflection. Revolutionaries do not procrastinate and avoid making decisions by perpetually weighing the possible results of various courses of action. Kierkegaard writes, "The environment, the contemporary age, has neither events nor integrated passion but in a negative unity creates a reflective opposition that toys for a moment with the unreal prospect and then resorts to the brilliant equivocation that the smartest thing has been done, after all, by doing nothing" (TA, 69). For the cautious contemporary person, procrastination and perpetual reconsideration are strategic evasions of responsibility, motivated by fear of the consequences of action. For example, a citizen in the age of reflection is really a spectator who sets up committees to consider the costs and benefits of loyalty. But, Kierkegaard remarks, zealous partisans are actively loyal to a cause; they are actors rather than spectators of world-historical events. The age of revolution encourages courageous and decisive agents rather than grandiloquent spectators. Kierkegaard repeated this theme in his journals from 1847, complaining that contemporary liberals, unlike the genuine reformers of the past, are cowards who do not take risks (KJN 4, 114). Their technical skill in deliberation ironically exempts them from the inconvenience and the anxiety of reaching a decision.

## Constancy

The virtue of constancy is also fostered by the revolutionary age. The zeal of the French legation is not evanescent or episodic, as are the enthusiasms of the present age. Kierkegaard developed this theme by contrasting this constancy to the fickle spirit of the present age. He wrote, "The present age is essentially *a sensible, reflecting age, devoid of passion, flaring up in superficial, short-lived enthusiasm and prudentially relaxing into indolence*" (TA, 68). This age of reflection is susceptible to histrionic and ephemeral outbursts of energy, but the exuberant dreams and projects are then followed by torpor. The superficial enthusiasms of contemporary people are attempts to win the momentary approval of the "crowd" and conform to the ideological fads of the moment. Over against this, Kierkegaard lauded the constancy of the citizens of the age of revolution in willing one thing (TA, 39). The stability and durability of the ideal provides a basis for the stability and durability of a life devoted to it. The commitment to an ideal can mature into a permanent disposition that survives the fluctuations and uncertainties of fortune. For Claudine and the individuals in the French legation like Lusard, the commitment to the ideals of the revolution had solidified into an enduring character. Their lives exhibited commendable continuity and reliability.

## An Alternative Form of Political Community

Kierkegaard suggested that these virtues could form the basis of a political community of individuals who are united by individually adopted common ideals. He observed, "When individuals (each one individually) are essentially and passionately related to an idea and together are essentially related to the same idea, the relation is optimal and normative" (TA, 62). A plurality of individual decisions, all made with inwardness and passion, could converge in the birth of an ideal type of political body. Such a community would not only maintain the essential distance of inwardness between individuals but would also encourage individuals to value the type of community that preserves singularity. The individuals in a revolutionary age are not gluttonously close to one another, as if they were a bestial herd, because their ideal-mediated union preserves a respectful distance. Their cohesion is unity-in-difference rather than enmeshment. If such a political community were to exist, its ethos could help foster the virtues of devotion to an ideal, concern for others, and respect for individuality, all of which the religious life requires.

The passion of the revolutionary age must be seasoned by self-awareness, awareness of the social environment, and awareness of the movement's goals. In his journals Kierkegaard stressed the need to understand a situation, and not just mindlessly pursue novel developments. He wrote, "They storm the palace in Paris, an anonymous mass, that doesn't know what it wants, lacking a concrete thought" (KJN 4, 347). The "mob" stage of the French revolution, he criticizes, had no definite objective. So also in Denmark, he complained, rudderless King Fredrick VII got flustered when trying to accommodate a variety of vociferous conflicting interests. This mindless activity, devoid of well-conceived goals, is like proposing marriage in the heat of the moment when the individual does not know what he is doing.

## 10 The Vices of the Present Age

In the last half of his review Kierkegaard devotes even more attention to outlining the ways in which the present age feeds certain vices that impede the pursuit of religious subjectivity. Those polemics enable him to highlight the classic virtues that had been lost. Many of these endangered virtues were not those of the age of revolution but harkened back to a more traditional society.

## The Elimination of Concrete Differentia

One of his chief targets is contemporary liberalism's subversion of organic communities. The more genuine organic community of prior ages was a far cry from the abstract equality of citizens lionized by the present age. He grieved that now the present generation had eliminated individuals and social concretions in the name of numerical equality and abstract humanity (TA, 107–108). He notes: "Contemporaneity with actual persons, each of whom is someone, in the actuality of the moment and the actuality of the situation gives support to the single individual" (TA, 91). Interaction with actual persons is supportive of the development of inwardness, for individuals can become more earnest about the shape and direction of their own lives as they wrestle with their obligations to specific persons and their complex emotional ties to them (TA, 92). Modern culture, however, reduces individuals to an unreal mathematical equality, in which the particularity of persons is devalued and volatized. Other people become generic fellow citizens, all defined by nothing more than identical legal rights. The exposure of this vice suggests that the appreciation of particularity is a virtue, and that certain political formations can foster it.

## The Epidemic of Envy

According to Kierkegaard, the present age is contaminated with an even more corrosive vice: envy. Envy directed toward those who do dare to exhibit notable virtues and excellences has become widespread. The individual, defined in terms of legal rights, longs to maintain the status of being as good as everyone else and, therefore, is suspicious of anyone who disturbs the equality of the lowest common denominator. Envy, Kierkegaard observes, demands that everyone should be like all the others (TA, 82–84). Envy is the hostility of conformists to those individuals who refuse to be satisfied with mediocrity and homogeneity (TA, 82–83). The culture of the present age has elevated the need for social acceptance to the status of a highest good. The denizens of the age of reflection desperately want to fit in with all the other good little children, no matter what the content of their ephemeral enthusiasms might be. Envy was so troubling to Kierkegaard that he concluded that it had become the negatively unifying vice of a reflective age (TA, 81). Moreover, he feared that there was no longer any real national spirit in Denmark because of envy, implying that a national spirit would be something much to be desired (KJN, 223).

After writing *Two Ages* Kierkegaard returned to the issue of envy in his journals, bemoaning the fact that envy directed at any person of ability had become rampant in Denmark (KJN 4, 14). The theme of "fear" looms large in his notes from this period. Denmark's principal evils, he asserted, included envy and the concomitant fear of peers (KN 4, 255). He lamented that the Danes had become a people who had no fear of God but only of town gossip. Social life in Denmark had been dominated by a fear of being perceived as different. The new tyranny, he warned, was not the monarchy, but the all-controlling fear of others (KJN 4, 340). The virtue opposite this vice would be imperviousness to the approbation or condemnation of the environing society. Such a virtue would be inspired by the recognition that there should be "higher" concerns in life than acceptance by a fickle and shallow public.

## The Evils of Leveling

The phenomenon of "leveling," a lethal social danger, is the inevitable public enactment of envy. Kierkegaard asserts that a reflective and apathetic era necessarily engages in leveling. This process of leveling glorifies mediocrity and being average and seeks to undermine anyone who exhibits an excellence. It flourishes because the present age is oriented toward a bland equality of undistinguished persons, a purely negative equality. The only superiority that it recognizes is the mathematical superiority of large numbers of citizens. Leveling is insidious; it is an abstract power, controlled and directed by no one in particular (TA, 84). Kierkegaard worries that not even loyalty to a nation with its individual culture can halt leveling, for leveling is done in the name of abstract humanity and can claim precedence over nationality (TA, 87).

One of Kierkegaard's main objections to leveling is that it discourages intimate connections among individuals, for it obliterates their particularity (TA, 84–85). Social concretions are not valued because the citizen qua citizen becomes the primary identifying mark of a person. In any era, leveling's erosion of particularity can occur in different forms and to different degrees. Approximate leveling construes persons as members of a social class, a tribe, and so on, but not as unique individuals. Thorough-going leveling, which is worse, seeks to abstract everyone from all the concretions of actuality, such as regional dialect, social class, and local culture (TA, 90). Both varieties militate against the appreciation of the singularity of persons and attention to their unique needs. A more traditional society, cognizant of the diversity of social roles, is better equipped to foster the virtue of sensitivity to individual situations.

According to Kierkegaard the power of leveling encourages a pernicious set of vices. Denmark, he lamented in 1848, was beset with pettiness and mockery (including the mockery of Kierkegaard), for ridicule was targeted on those who were not impressed by the public's display of strength (KJN 4, 354). The population was susceptible to collective narcissism, based on no real merits, and was contemptuous of outsiders (KJN 4, 310). Kierkegaard mourned that provincialism and mean-spiritedness were spreading among the Danes. He remarked that the superficial jingoism evident during the prelude to the Schleswig-Holstein war was so potent that a person would be suspected of being German if he did not wear a certain kind of hat. The fear of Germany was a fantasy, he claimed, calculated to bolster the delusion that Denmark must be a great nation if it had such powerful enemies (KJN 4, 310). In the present age the crowd transforms political allegiances into mere self-serving markers of tribal identity.

## The Corrosive Effects of Chatter and Publicity

Along similar lines Kierkegaard condemns the pervasive culture of "chatter." Chatter is a most pernicious and subtle vice because it subverts the development of earnestness (TA, 97–100). Kierkegaard observes that the public's chatter annuls the distinction of the significant and the trivial, and even the concern for truth and falsity. With chatter there are no important events to speak about, for any topic, no matter how inconsequential, can attract attention. In Denmark the public/private boundary has been abolished, and superficial gossip about individuals' personal lives proliferates (TA, 100). Constantly mutating trends and fads propagated by the popular media are determining the individual's fluctuating interests. Consequently, people's enthusiasms are essentially about nothing and nothing decisive was meant by them. According to Kierkegaard, chatter is the negation of the crucial distinction between silence and speaking (TA, 97).

Sentences are articulated, as in speech, but nothing significant is said, as in silence. Chatter involves a disjunction of the communicative form and the empty content. Silence, Kierkegaard claimed, is the condition for cultured conversation between persons, for only silence can preserve the difference between what is important and what is not (TA, 99). Authentic communication, Kierkegaard reminds his readers, is not trivial prattling or gossiping. The extensive range of chatter is counterproductive for religion because people talk about everything. Opposed to this, the inwardness of the religious life requires silence to focus on the one thing that should be willed.

Closely related to Kierkegaard's condemnation of "chatter" is his critique of "publicity," which is the contemporary enactment of chatter on a societal scale (TA, 70). In contrast to the age of revolutionary action, Kierkegaard condemns his present age for being an era of miscellaneous announcements. In the public arena, people talk about every issue, devoid of conviction and even of real interest (TA, 101). Given the absence of heart-felt projects and commitments, public announcements are merely an amusing distraction, intended to keep boredom at bay (TA, 70). As with chatter, public loquaciousness is the negation of the disjunction of the significant and the trivial (TA, 97). The range of topics is extensive, but none of them are explored intensively. The public may be familiar with a great deal of information, and be well-informed, but in the absence of passionate concern about anything the ability to judge the relative importance of bits of data is subverted.

Chatter and publicity spawn the danger of unrestrained relativism. Kierkegaard complains that the crowd could be interested in the establishment of a brothel, or it could be just as easily interested in the new hymn book (TA, 102). If the "demands of the times" determine value, then anything could be a temporary matter of ultimate concern. The absence of any "inner drive of enthusiasm" removes any standard for judging which values are most important, and which issues are worthy of most investigation (TA, 101). Kierkegaard observed that the popular abstract phrase "on principle" can be applied to anything and justify any course of action. One can object to wearing orange cravats "on principle," and one can object to mandatory infant baptism "on principle." A relativistic culture, with no sense of the comparative gravity of issues, subverts the development of the single-mindedness that the religious life requires.

## Voyeurism, Exhibitionism, and Pretense

According to Kierkegaard, a vicious consequence of chatter and publicity is the upsurge in voyeurism. Both in private conversations and public assemblies, the present age is a culture of observation, not action (TA, 74). The public observes because it is bored; individuals look for titillation and distraction from the vacuity of their own lives (TA, 136). Being a spectator has the added benefit of supporting inaction (TA, 73). Kierkegaard observes that now the citizen is primarily a detached spectator contemplating a problem, for example, the relation of the subject to the king, rather than trying to be a loyal countryman (TA, 78–79). Similarly, going to school does not mean becoming educated, but being more or less interested in the problem of education. No longer do fathers exert authority and sons respond with defiance. Rather, now the two observe each other and ponder the issue of their relationship. The relationship lacks the inwardness and intensity that could make the child's obedience and the father's authority concrete and fruitful (TA, 80). Kierkegaard proposes sarcastically that observers could even form committees to discuss their observations. The vice of voyeurism is an abdication of responsibility. Kierkegaard avers that the voyeur can take delight in the sight of a nasty dog attacking a superior person, but assume no responsibility for the dog (TA, 95). The spectator, safe in snobbish indolence, can observe the vicissitudes of a superior person for as long as the observation continues to be amusing. Such emotional distancing from actuality is inimical to the responsible engagement with existence that the religious life presupposes.

The present age also encourages the vice of exhibitionism, the flip-side of voyeurism. (TA, 102). The exhibitionist tendency is the product of the self-infatuation that is a reaction to the collapse of organic communities. The contextual "givens" of one's identity are not ascribed by tradition and one's social role; rather, identity is a self-generated performance. This valorization of self-creation is made possible by the press's abolition of the public/private distinction (TA, 100). The superficiality and artificiality of self-presentation in the contemporary age relies upon the negation of the distinction between private hiddenness and public revelation, erasing the private sphere. In the present age an individual's public persona is an artifice that is intended to be mistaken for reality. In such an environment of illusory façades, it would be exceedingly difficult to cultivate the self-concern that religious inwardness must include.

In a related way, the widespread vice of pretense infects the present age. Pretense robs institutions of their potency and substance, but retains their empty forms. An age of reflection pretending to be revolutionary "lets everything remain but subtly drains the meaning out of it," thereby making responsible action impossible (TA, 77). For example, contemporary Danes do not want to abolish the monarchy overtly, but little-by-little they seek to turn it into a ceremonial ornament, devoid of real authority (TA, 80–81). Kierkegaard excoriates those who want to turn the monarchy into make-believe (TA, 80–81), for that charade encourages a comfort level with dissimulation. Danes allow the external trappings of the established order to continue but are fully aware of their fictive nature. The elegant book cover and the tawdry text inside do not match. Everyone is aware of the masquerade, but no one acknowledges it. This sort of deception habituates a population to indulgence in sleights-of-hand, in which political life becomes theater. Over against this, the religious life requires ruthless honesty, not collective self-delusion.

## The Plague of Shrewdness

A cognate vice of the present age is shrewdness. Kierkegaard sadly observes that in contemporary Denmark even children are shrewd (TA, 68). Shrewdness is motivated by the realization that ambition, greed, and self-aggrandizement are honored by society (TA, 78). A shrewd person turns her back on the good and devotes her life to the pursuit of earthly benefits. Kierkegaard writes, "The distinction between good and evil is enervated by a loose, supercilious, theoretical acquaintance with evil, by an overbearing shrewdness which knows that the good is not rewarded or appreciated in this world – and thus it practically becomes stupidity" (TA 78). This shrewd worldliness requires the prudential calculation of the correlation of means to ends, and the pragmatic weighing of the pros and cons of various courses of action (TA, 68). According to Kierkegaard shrewdness exhibits a high degree of extensivity, infecting every dimension of life. The shrewd use of pragmatic means-to-ends analysis is most obvious in the economic sphere, but it permeates everything. Kierkegaard cautions that it has invaded political life, draining politics of inwardness and enthusiasm. Shrewdness has even corrupted domesticity and religion with cost-benefit calculation (TA, 73–74). Kierkegaard says, "In the present age not even the spontaneity of erotic love is as carefree as the lily of the field and in the lovers' eyes more glorious than Solomon in all his glory' (TA, 75). Such anxious shrewdness always militates against the risk-taking and willingness to sacrifice worldly goods that the religious life requires.

## Vicious Cultural Phenomena: The Public and the Crowd

In his literary review Kierkegaard ascribes the proliferation of these vices to certain specific sociopolitical phenomena and institutions. One of the most nefarious of the non-institutional phenomena is "the public" (TA, 90–95). The "public" is the product of the interaction of invisible and non-identifiable sources of opinions, gossip, and fads with a passive, irresponsible audience. The essential peril confronting Denmark, Kierkegaard claimed, was this "monstrous abstraction," the "victory" of social disembodiment (TA, 90). Unlike a political party or a people, the public is not a concretion; in fact, it obliterates all concrete forms of real sociability (TA, 108). Nor is the public like a congregation, for congregations are what they are by being concretions. According to Kierkegaard, the public is not even like a nation, for in this degenerate age a person can critique a whole nation in the name of the ethereal public (TA, 93). The public is an anonymous, faceless nothing, an abstraction with no conscience or intentional decision-making capacity. The public arises only when there is no strong communal life to provide any antidote. The growth of the public occurs in tandem with the valorization of the citizen as defined by legal rights, for in both cases organic connections have been replaced by numerical equality. The public, like all undifferentiated and impersonal structures, is an egregiously alienating phenomenon, undermining the self-assumption of responsibility that the religious life presupposes.

Elaborating the vices that "the public" encourages, Kierkegaard bitterly observes that "a generation, a nation, a general assembly, a community, a man can know shame for fickleness and disloyalty, but a public remains the public" (TA, 92). As a phantom, its center of consciousness and volition cannot be located, for it has none. Even with approximate publics, such as the dissolution of individual identities into the nation, something can be identified that is creating the public mass consciousness, such as the propaganda office of a government (TA, 91). But with the public, there is no institutional agency that can be pinpointed. The public is an amorphous non-entity, positioned nowhere in particular but operating everywhere. The public is morally and ideologically protean and has no permanent values to give it solidity. In spite of its spectral quality, Kierkegaard feared that contemporary Danes were deferring to this chimera, obeying it as the propagator of faddish opinions and the arbiter of taste, to whose dictates everyone must mindlessly conform.

The public for Kierkegaard epitomizes political and cultural phenomena that can only engender vices and undercut growth in religious virtues. A culture that lionizes the public encourages the individual to abdicate personal responsibility for making decisions of existential importance. Kierkegaard claims that in ancient times the people had to bear responsibility for public action and had to come forward in person in public meetings (TA, 91). But now the amoral public persuades the pseudo-citizens to huddle together and collectively shirk genuine political accountability.

For Kierkegaard "the crowd" was the visible, social embodiment of the public. It was the congealing of indistinct people into glutinous social masses, like clubs and political parties. A crowd can be as abstract as the readership of specific newspapers or as concrete as a mob at a rally. Kierkegaard's contempt for the crowd was boundless. In journal entries from 1847 he warned that it is not the government that is a tyrant, but the crowd (KJN 4, 142). He declared that in the contemporary age authentic reformers who detest despotism must oppose not the monarchy, but the crowd (KJN 4, 135). The new style of tyrant is not one person, but a vicious conglomerate, a many-headed hydra (KJN 4, 143). For Kierkegaard, allowing one's identity to be dissolved into the crowd was a cardinal vice that was inimical to the religious life's assumption of personal accountability.

## Vicious Institutions: The Press

Kierkegaard proposes that certain institutions do promote the viciousness of the public and the crowd. According to Kierkegaard a major institution through which the vices of the present age are propagated is the press. The press, like the public that it had helped create, is also an abstraction, for it has no center of consciousness and responsibility and exhibits no cohesive action (TA, 93). He exclaims that it is the abuse of the press that has shattered Denmark (KJN 4, 305). Because of the press, he mourned, the state was now demoralized (KJN 6, 27), and both the state and Christianity were becoming impossibilities (KJN 7, 184, 226). Given his controversy with the *Corsair* in 1846 while he was writing the literary review, Kierkegaard was painfully cognizant of the press' deleterious power.

Kierkegaard's distaste for contemporary journalism had a long history, dating back to 1834 when he expressed reservations about the freedom of the press and its pretentions in his first published literary piece. Throughout his career Kierkegaard's complaints about the press multiplied and intensified. First, he grumbled that liberal journalism just talked about abuses, not about institutional solutions (KJN, 11 1, 196 ff.). Second, the anonymity of the essays in the newspapers and journals allowed authors to make sensationalistic claims without responsibility. With the cloak of anonymity anything could be said by anybody about anybody, no matter how scurrilous and irresponsible it might be. Third, journals like *Kobenhavnpost* were not examples of political action but were exercises in cowardice. The heated words in its pages did not come spontaneously from the heart but were coolly calculated to provoke the government while avoiding trouble with the censors. True literary action, however, should take the risk of making the author vulnerable to reprisals through passionate polemical outbursts. In general, liberal journalism has taken credit for inspiring and energizing reform movements, but it has not been as influential as it pretends to be. Fourth, journals like the *Kobenshavnpost* exhibited no ideological unity. Rather than presenting a coherent political vision, they expressed countervailing liberal and conservative trajectories. Their articles were not thoughtful articulations of a unifying idea. Far from encouraging coherent action, the press fostered a fussy busyness. According to Kierkegaard, the authors in the liberal press were great cowards who only know how to talk, without committing themselves to any public action (KJN 4, 114).

All these criticisms suggest that the press has become a fertilizer for certain vices that inhibit the development of a healthy civic life. The press, Kierkegaard warns, is a soporific that tranquilizes self-reflection and stifles concern about the shape of one's own life and the assumption of responsibility for it (TA, 80). It fosters a carping whininess that is more interested in criticizing other individuals and institutions than it is in taking constructive action. It encourages the cowardice of attacking others without fear of consequences. In general, it inhibits the development of the responsible, coherent, unified vision of life that religious existence needs in order to flourish.

Of course, Kierkegaard did not develop these cursory critical reflections into a full-blown political theory. He explicitly disclaimed any interest in political philosophy (LD, 255). He resisted identifying himself with any of the current programs of political reform (PV, 18–19). Accordingly, in his response to Andreas G. Rudelbach he railed against Denmark's disastrous confusion of politics and Christianity (CO, 53). Kierkegaard's chief concern remained the recovery of what he took to be authentic Christianity and the catalyzing of passionate concern for the shape of one's own life.

## Subjectivity-promoting Political Cultures

Nevertheless, this concern to protect and promote religious subjectivity did motivate him to explicitly articulate some characteristics that a healthy political system should possess. He did more than suggest that a religiously apt political order would discourage the vices of the present age that impede the development of true inwardness. His review's blistering critique of the present age did not culminate in utter indifference to political entities, despair over the possible value of political movements, or a condemnation of all forms of political association. Rather, the novel inspired him to cautiously imagine a mode of political life that could actually encourage the virtues necessary for the religious life.

We have seen that Kierkegaard did applaud the passion of the French legation, while not necessarily endorsing all of its ideological values. The legation, as a political entity, was subjectivity-promoting. Beyond this, Kierkegaard did suggest in a piecemeal way that other political associations, besides revolutionary factions, could encourage the growth of virtues that are relevant for the religious life. The test of their validity was their capacity to promote such virtues.

For example, Kierkegaard lauded the unique values of at least some monarchical polities. His approbation of monarchy was an intensification of his the more generalized support of the state. In this literary review he explicitly advocated the virtue of loyalty to the king (TA, 78–79). In substantial communal life the people participate in the identity of the king who represents them and must accept personal accountability for his actions. Consequently, the individuals who comprise the nation should experience corporate guilt when the monarch is disloyal to the nation's ideals. Kierkegaard concludes that participation in the national spirit can foster a sense of shame when the regime is fickle and untrue to its own values, for the regime is the embodiment of the citizenry (TA, 92). Besides outrage when the monarch acts tyrannically, loyalty to the monarch encourages cheerful approbation when the regime acts justly (TA 78–79). A sense of responsibility is fostered as individuals learn to accept the consequences of the state's actions even when they disagree with the state's policies. To share the values of a nation is to be exposed with fellow citizens to the possibility of corporate guilt. The acceptance of such risk can become an upbuilding pedagogy in moral responsibility.

For Kierkegaard, loyalty to the monarch also fosters the important virtue of dutiful respect for a norm. In a journal entry from 1847 Kierkegaard suggested that an absolute monarchy when functioning properly accustoms people to obedience to an ideal requirement (KJN 4, 261). Of course, this obedience must be a function of the personal internalization of the ideal requirement, and not grudging submission to external power. This practice in dedication to an ideal requirement was crucial for the development of religious subjectivity; the political virtue could be transferred to the religious sphere.

Kierkegaard also gestured toward the virtues that even non-monarchial states could encourage. The state can also foster the consciousness that the individual occupies a position within the social fabric and should perform her socially beneficial roles responsibly. In his journals Kierkegaard lamented that in the present age a sense of duty had been replaced by equivocating deliberation and the hunger for power. The youth of Denmark knew nothing of duty, he wrote, which made the development of religious virtues much more difficult for them than it should be.

Moreover, Kierkegaard did not hesitate to applaud the aspects of any national culture that could promote robust action. In 1848 Kierkegaard complained that his contemporary culture propagated the pernicious attitude that just by yelling about being a patriot one becomes one. In opposition to this he remarked, "I thought that one became a patriot by being a patriot, and that was that" (KJN 11.2, 184). He sarcastically observed that now a hallmark of being patriotic is the willingness to condemn those who run a bowling alley because bowling alleys are associated with German culture (KJN 11.2, 185). A spirit of active patriotism can encourage virtues that would support a life of active faith, rather than empty espousals of belief. Neither formulaic avowals of patriotism nor merely verbal consent to doctrinal systems possess the requisite willingness to act that would qualify them as being genuine.

## The Virtues and Vices of Denmark

Kierkegaard did not hesitate to display his particular attachment to Denmark, and the value of this attachment. In a journal entry from 1847 Kierkegaard exclaimed, "how careful it [Denmark] ought to be with the goodness and excellence that it possesses" (KJN 4, 166). He sprinkles his review with the affectionate phrase "little Denmark" (TA, 42). For example, he celebrates the anonymous author's "conscious and contented joy over little Denmark" (TA, 16). "Little" in this context is approbative, for Kierkegaard opines that for his vision of a society of genuine individuals cooperating with one another to be viable, the state must be very small. Moreover, he delights that the novel is written in Danish, and congratulated the author's "faithful adherence to a Danish reading public" (TA, 16). The fact that the Danish reading public was so small had a beneficial dimension, for it promoted a cozy, intimate relationship of the author and the readers, with the author providing a new story every Christmas season, as if it were a gift (TA, 17). Even though the author was anonymous, the author/reader relationship was not abstract. Denmark should take advantage of the fact that it was geographically difficult to leave the country, for that concentrated the citizens' sense of responsibility for its well-being. He even rejoiced that Copenhagen was the only real city in the country, for that reduced the center of culture to a manageable scale. (As is well known, very soon Kierkegaard's social ostracism would motivate him to disparage Copenhagen, routinely calling it a coarse "market town.")

Part of Kierkegaard's appreciation of Denmark was simply due to the fact that it happened to be his own nation.[42] This appreciation for one's local culture and one's compatriots, simply because they are at hand, parallels Claudine's delight in the neighbors among whom she has been accidentally thrown. The ability to accept the unique features of one's situation as a gift from providence is a virtue highlighted in many of Kierkegaard's upbuilding discourses (EUD 31–48, 114–157). That virtue can be intentionally cultivated and savored. Such appreciation for the particularities of an individual's given circumstances is a potent pedagogy in gratitude.

Even Kierkegaard's often scathing criticisms of contemporary Denmark presupposed an appreciation of its former virtues and a hope for the possibility of recovering them. His often acerbic critiques were partly based on a retrospective evaluation of what Denmark had been and could still be. When he mourned the demoralization of Denmark and the new spread of the servile spirit of pettiness, gossip, and libel, he implied that this was a decline from a former more admirable state (KJN 11.2, 163). As the Schleswig-Holstein war approached, Kierkegaard remarked that Denmark now pretended to be one of the great powers, while it formerly had a more salutary, humble self-understanding (KJN 11.2, 236). Kierkegaard complained that Denmark had become crazy enough to try to be like Paris, implying that it had not always harbored such delusional aspirations

---

[42] A similar argument is advanced by Casey Spinks, "Faith in the Commonplace: The Knight of Faith in Local Community," *Perspectives in Religious Studies*, 46(1) (2019): 29–37. Spinks argues against conflating Kierkegaard's criticisms of nationalism with a thoroughgoing rejection of organic local cultures.

(KJN 4, 391). Denmark, he observed in 1847, imagined itself to be embattled with the whole world for the sake of its nationality, but in reality it was corroded with envy and scarcely resembled a people any longer (KJN 4, 148). Kierkegaard's use of "any longer" implies that until recently it actually had been a people. Similarly, his remark that "soon the Danish people will no longer be a nation, but a flock" suggested that Denmark still was a nation, and that being a nation was a desirable thing (KJN 4, 123). He wrote in a journal entry probably from 1848 that it was a new phenomenon that chatter was now submerging the country and might ruin it (KJN 11.2, 238). The spread of such palaver must be prevented in order to "rescue something that could be called public opinion" (KJN 11.2, 240). Imagining that a European statesman was defending freedom of the press as a necessary evil, Kierkegaard exhorted his fellow citizens: "Then tell him that, up there in the north, there lies a land blessed by nature in every way, a happy talented little people," but then that nation had unwisely introduced the press (KJN 11, pt. 2, 239). Kierkegaard's lamentations about the rise of the "rabble" are only intelligible if it is assumed that in the past healthier organic communities had been the norm (KJN 11.2, 240). He admitted that he had been wrong about Denmark, having imagined that the vulgarity of the mob was not the true public spirit, but now he realized that crudity and vulgarity reigned in Copenhagen, where everyone sought their own advantage (KJN 4, 122). That vulgarity had not always been the case, for he opined that "Ppl. are not evil but have gone astray; it is important that they should become aware" (KJN 4, 123). As late as 1850 Kierkegaard still expressed this hope, "Oh, that I were now able, as I wished, to move every single Dane to at least love his native land so as not to will its ruin with diabolical violence and power" (KJN 11.2, 240). Clearly in his view at the time, love of one's country, simply because it is one's country, is not a vice, but has positive potential for the development of religiously relevant virtues.

Kierkegaard's approbative attitude toward love of country is evident in his hope that the sorry spiritual condition of Denmark could be remedied, even though that would be painful. He remarked that the nation's "wretchedness will be revealed," and that Denmark "needs to see this revelation" in order to be rehabilitated (KJN 4, 188). Kierkegaard attested that he aspired to contribute to the revitalization of his nation, writing in 1847 that he confronted the new ethos of vulgarity "just to do my bit in protecting the good spirit of Denmark, so that it in turn can protect, favor, and encourage its true children, instead of sacrificing them in an idolatry serving an un-Danish spirit" (KJN 4, 258). Although he complained that no one really read his books in Denmark, but only alluded to them to display a fashionable sophistication, he declared that "I fight for the honor of the language and the literature" (KJN 4, 147).

## The Reform of Institutions

Kierkegaard did not discount the fact that the reform of institutions could remove unnecessary impediments to the development of the virtues essential for the religious life. Although he insisted that living before God was a possibility open to all individuals, no matter what their social location, he was also convinced that certain social practices and institutions promoted obstacles like smug elitism and unreflective conformism. Most significantly, in 1847 he advocated a tighter governmental regulation of the press. Journals like the *Corsair* embittered one social class against another and made it difficult to cultivate love for the neighbor. Kierkegaard identified the press's penchant for libelous *ad hominem* attacks and scurrilous gossip as one of the primary motors energizing the phenomenon of levelling. To mitigate this, the government could restrain the excesses of the daily press (KJN 4, 150). In 1847 he wrote:

> The government cannot outlaw the natural powers that a man possesses, but it can forbid the possession of firearms because these are much too powerful and beyond the domain of the human. In the same way, the government cannot prohibit spoken communication, which is a gift of God, but it could very well prohibit the daily press, because it is far too powerful as a means of communication. The printing of notices and advertisements might be permitted, but no form of argumentation should appear in the daily press. (KJN 4, 150)

For Kierkegaard another example of a hurtful institutional structure was the proposal of the populists to transform the church into a bureaucratic institution overseen by the constitutional state. This arrangement would exacerbate the tendency to amalgamate faith and nationalism that had already been a problem under the absolute monarchy. The separation of the church and the state, particularly their financial separation, could counteract this cultural proclivity, something which Kierkegaard increasingly emphasized.

According to Kierkegaard, particular institutions and practices of the church, the state, and the culture had artificially increased the already formidable difficulty of cultivating inwardness. These impediments had been created by human beings and therefore could be critiqued, resisted, and perhaps dismantled by human beings. His writings in 1846 and 1847 suggested that the institutions that encouraged these onerous obstacles to genuine selfhood could be changed and should be changed, even though that would be a daunting and even frightening task.

It must be admitted that Kierkegaard's interest in changing political structures was limited and severely qualified. Although he did advocate for the reform of institutions like the press, more often he emphasized the need for the religious awakening of individuals as the ultimate remedy for the corruption of Denmark.

According to Kierkegaard, vices like reflection, envy, irresponsibility, and conformism were so entrenched in the present age that liberation from them required
a radical remediation. Only the appreciation of the religious equality of all
individuals *coram deo* could counteract the corrupting impact of leveling and
enable the creation of true community. He remarks that there is no task as difficult
as extricating oneself from the temptations of reflection, especially when social
institutions stimulate and reinforce it (TA, 77). Kierkegaard writes:

> for if the individual is unwilling to be satisfied with himself in the essentiality
> of the religious life before God, to be satisfied with ruling over himself
> instead of over the world, to be satisfied as a pastor to be his own audience,
> as an author to be his own reader, etc., if he is unwilling to learn to be inspired
> by this as supreme because it expresses equality before God and equality with
> all men, then he will not escape from reflection. (TA, 89)

In the final analysis, only the embrace of religious inwardness could revive the
category of the individual and counteract the self's dissolution. Accordingly, in
his journals of 1847 Kierkegaard warned, "If crudity is not to overtake Denmark
there must be an awakening" (KJN, 317). Before this awakening can happen,
individual Danes must go through a period of agonized self-examination and
repentance. According to Kierkegaard, the current cultural/political malaise
could only be healed by the awakening of individuals.

For Kierkegaard these awakenings could also be described as the revitalization
of ethical and religious life-views. Such life-views were a *sine qua non* of "uniting"
into genuine civil communities. He wrote pointedly, "Not until the single individual has established a new ethical stance despite the whole world, not until then can
there be any question of uniting" (TA, 106). The problem with the health of any
sort of "association" is that is ultimately a religious problem, or, more precisely, the
problem of creating a society that would be conducive to the cultivation of
religious inwardness. However, this claim that the ultimate remedy for
Denmark's ills is the awakening of individual Danes does not negate the possibility
that the reform of institutions like the press could help promote that awakening.

## The Martyr's Pedagogy

A concluding theme in Kierkegaard's review also pointed to the virtue-shaping
power of the cultural and political environment, but in a paradoxical way.
Kierkegaard entertained the hope that the pervasive superficiality of the present
age could indirectly promote deeper inwardness. As the cultural vices became
more blatant and undeniable, their overt perniciousness could motivate individuals to cultivate their own inwardness. For example, Kierkegaard speculated
that God may permit leveling in order to stimulate a hunger for higher forms of

life (TA, 109). In this way it is possible for a person to be negatively educated by leveling. Kierkegaard wrote, "Yet by means of it [levelling] every individual, each one separately, may in turn be religiously educated, in the highest sense may be helped to acquire the essentiality of the religious by means of the *examen rigorosum* [rigorous examination] of levelling" (TA, 87). Moreover, if individuals could be made aware of the dangers of reflection, shrewdness, leveling, and the crowd mentality, and could be encouraged to feel the sting of their liabilities, then the creation of a community of genuine individuals would be possible. The present age with its political ethos could educate by repelling a person, clearing the way for more salubrious forms of association. Interestingly, even this possibility of negative education still presupposes that political and cultural formations can either encourage or impede the growth of certain spiritually relevant virtues and vices. In this case the pedagogy operates as a reaction against the vices of the present age.

Another consideration complicated Kierkegaard's assessment of the possibilities for reforming the political and cultural situation. The reform of this present culture of leveling must be indirect. Because the vices of the present age include conformism and the abnegation of personal responsibility, the contemporary malaise cannot be healed through a direct assertion of coercive authority. Such an attempt to dominate others ideologically would simply reinforce the tendency to submit to an external authority to which the individual must conform. Such a self-defeating strategy would militate against the individual's assumption of responsibility for her own life.

Kierkegaard concluded that any contemporary leader of reform must educate indirectly by suffering at the hands of the crowd (TA, 109). A reformer could ensure that this suffering would be visited upon him simply by publicly refusing to live by the crowd's norms. The exposure of the crowd's vicious hostility toward anyone who dared to challenge its vices could catalyze widespread self-critical reflection and individual repentance. In other words, Kierkegaard was advocating social martyrdom as a pedagogical strategy, a theme that would become increasingly pronounced in his later writings. Repentant individuals could then form a voluntary counter-cultural community that would nurture the virtues necessary for the religious life. It is important to note that in *Two Ages* Kierkegaard was advancing this as a strategy to remediate the political/cultural malaise, and not just as a plan of action to reform the individual. A resultant political community could then engage in virtue education more directly.

A caveat is in order here. After the political turmoil of 1848, Kierkegaard's assessment of the cultural situation of Denmark became increasingly pessimistic as he became convinced that the power of the church and the state was being used to make the Christian life impossible. He was progressively alarmed by

Denmark's growing desire to mimic other nations, the burgeoning power of the "crowd," the state's willingness to subordinate Christianity to popular opinion through the "people's church," and the failure of the church to confess its sins. In December 1854 he published an article in *The Fatherland*, "Was Bishop Mynster a Truth-Witness?" that excoriated the conflation of being "a witness for the truth" with having a successful ecclesial career and social approbation (TM, 3–8). In his final years Kierkegaard wondered if Christianity might be so intrinsically asocial that it cannot justify the existence any type of congregation. Perhaps religious earnestness and life in community are incompatible. The nation's purpose to make life easy is at odds with Christianity's call to suffer for the truth. Both the church and the state obscure a clear vision of the demands of the Christian life and undermine authentic striving to actualize the ideal. Even if such an extreme anti-communal sentiment is a plausible construal of Kierkegaard's late attack litera-ture, such a conclusion is not suggested by his literary review of 1846.

The concluding pages of *Two Ages* suggest that Denmark's basic problem is not something specific like agrarian unrest, a decline in shipping, the monarchy, or the impending Schleswig-Holstein War. Moreover, the predicament confronting the present age is not the essential nature of romance, the family, or even the nation as such. The fundamental ailment of the present age is the rise of a mass society that is paralyzed by reflection and conformism. This cultural contagion had infected romantic relations, the family, the state, the church, and all social institutions. The idolization of the mercurial crowd had robbed all forms of relationality of their power to nurture the virtues necessary for inwardness. According to Kierkegaard, the politics and cultural sensibilities of the present age were an exercise in self-deification disguised by bourgeois respectability and hollow piety. Most basically, the valorization of conformity and reflective inaction militated against the passionate self-responsibility that both the religious life and social life demand. Although the vices of modernity were deeply embedded in particular institutions and practices, Kierkegaard cherished the hope that the corrupting ethos, practices, and institutions of the present age could be resisted and reformed.

## 11 Conclusion

Kierkegaard's treatment of the issue of the relation of social and interpersonal bonds to the development of religious inwardness was highly nuanced and dialectical, even in the writings from the limited period of 1846–1848. It is understandable that the complexity would spawn divergent interpretive trajec-tories. On the one hand, critics and expositors from Martensen to Krishek are right to stress Kierkegaard's discomfort with the natural loves, including romance. Kierkegaard's description of love for the neighbor does raise serious questions about preferential attachments. Moreover, interpreters from Adorno to Backhouse are right to emphasize Kierkegaard's antipathy not only to nationalism, but also his suspicion of just about any form of political association. Kierkegaard's misgivings about the stultifying power of collectivities did run deep. On the other hand, interpreters like Ferreira, Lippett, and Maranduic are right to discern in Kierkegaard's writings a way of positively valuing certain forms of the natural loves.

Both the disjunctive and the conjunctive trajectories are evident in *Two Ages* itself. However, the most singular thing about his literary review is that Kierkegaard suggested a way of relating *agape* and the natural loves that does not fit either of these textual patterns or the interpretive traditions they spawned. He intimated that some forms of romantic and political relationships could serve as a pedagogy in the virtues that the religious life presupposes. He affirmed this possibility overtly in regard to romance, particularly in his qualified preference for the romance typical of the age of revolution. He also strongly implied the spiritually salutary potentialities of certain forms of civil associations. These potentialities are suggested not only by his explicit statements, but also by the fact that the novel's plot assumes that romantic relationships are significantly shaped by political climates, sometimes in good ways. Consequently, his appreciation (and critique) of the one can be transferred to the other. The two varieties of social attachments share a common ability to aid the development of the virtues that religion requires.

It must be admitted that political and social concerns were always secondary or tertiary for Kierkegaard. Even in 1846 they were only important to him in so far as they promoted or impeded the development of the virtues relevant for the religious life. Qualifying the importance of political and cultural concerns, he often insisted that religious subjectivity could be chosen and cultivated by an individual under any political regime or cultural ethos. For example, in *Upbuilding Discourses in Various Spirits*, after noting the pedagogical potential of romance for the religious life, Kierkegaard reminded the reader, "it (romance) can be omitted without losing the highest; it can be missed without having lost the highest!" (UDVS, 109). Romance is neither a necessary nor a sufficient condition for religious growth. The same can be said of participation in civic associations.

Kierkegaard's positive assessment of certain kinds of romance and political organization was qualified by his apprehension of the capacity of all forms of sociality to squelch inwardness. Pernicious forms of romance and political allegiances can encourage conformism, envy, the narrowing of ethical concern, the abdication of responsibility, subservience to popular opinion, and the valorization of mediocrity. For this reason, Kierkegaard loathed both the mandarin culture of Denmark's Golden Age and the populist idolization of national and ethnic culture. He scorned the elitism of Mynster, the ethnocentricity of Grundtvig, the paternalism of Clausen, and the relativism of Lehmann. The various expressions of these parties all endorsed some form of *Sittlichheit*, whether that be Grundtvig's amalgam of Nordic culture and Christianity, Mynster's conflation of faith and high culture, Clausen's anti-absolutist liberalism, Martensen's glorification of the national church, or Lehman's romanticization of the spirit of the people. His sweeping criticisms of all factions makes it difficult to assimilate Kierkegaard's political and cultural sensibilities to any standard category. His review of *Two Ages* was neither an endorsement of anti-liberal reaction nor a call for populist reform. Kierkegaard in 1846 was not a liberal, nor was he a conservative.

Against all factions and movements, Kierkegaard's consistent contention was that Danish communal life was not an ultimate good and should not be conflated with Christianity. No collective consciousness or devotion to a lover should be allowed to overwhelm the self-responsibility and inwardness of the individual that are essential aspects of true religiosity. Kierkegaard consistently opposed all threats to the flourishing of subjectivity, including those posed by the state and romance. Kierkegaard's nonnegotiable conviction was that everyone must make the leap into religious subjectivity by themselves (TA, 108–109).

Despite this important qualification, in 1846 Kierkegaard was by no means indifferent to political and social matters. Although Kierkegaard was convinced that the only ultimate remedy for the ills of the present age would be the individual's cultivation of religious inwardness, this did not negate his appreciation of the ability of social and cultural conditions to either promote or hinder this inwardness. Spiritually healthy forms of civic association could protect the ability of the individual to engage in such cultivation. At their best, forms of civic association could even help form the virtues that genuine faith presupposes.

The basic point of the polemical last half of his literary review was that a particular political or cultural formation can engender vicious dispositions that are inimical to the cultivation of religious subjectivity. Although faith can be chosen in any context, some contexts needlessly make that choice more difficult than others. Certain features of social, cultural, and political life can encourage vices that impede the development of faith in ways that are not necessary. At the very least, Kierkegaard hoped that the critique of the dominant political sensibility and the reform of the institutions that supported it could minimize these obstructions.

The vices that the present age encourages include the escapist resort to reflection, the unwillingness to cultivate passion, the resistance to taking risks, the conformity to collective sensibilities, fickleness, envy, and worldly shrewdness. The pernicious dynamics that are operative in the public sphere and in interpersonal relationships make dispositions like shame, moral outrage, and a hunger for righteousness exceedingly difficult to cultivate. In *Two Ages* it is institutions and phenomena like the public, reflection, economic prudence, the press, and the amalgamation of church and state that promote the evaporation of the individual into an insubstantial vapor. But, Kierkegaard hoped, the power of such artificial obstacles could be mitigated and perhaps could even be removed.

This possibility gestures toward the theme that a political and cultural climate different from that of the present age would be more conducive to the flourishing of religiously relevant virtues. Such a climate should also avoid the impulsiveness of the age of revolution. Kierkegaard implied that society can be reformed to promote religiously relevant virtues, and not just to remove impediments. In the midst of his frequent critiques of the natural forms of attachment, he simultaneously suggested that romance and political associations of certain sorts can serve a positive role in the development of faith. They can function as a pedagogy in the virtues that faith presupposes and by which faith is continuously supported.

The desirable virtues that could be invigorated include passionate devotion to ideals, inwardness, self-reflection, concern for the shape of one's life as a whole, the assumption of responsibility, fidelity to long-term commitments, and the willingness to take risks. Even the age of reflection's realistic assessment of possibilities and situations would be a valuable virtue. Whether or not a distinct form of romance or political ethos can serve as a preparatory pedagogy for the religious life depends on its specific features and its specific context.

For Kierkegaard during this period something more than exhortations about self-sustained inward transformation could support the development of virtuous dispositions. Not only should the spirit of the times in the abstract be modified, but so also should be its concrete organs and instrumentalities. For example, a reform of the institutional structures that empower the crowd and the public would be beneficial. The outrages of the press could be restrained. Christianity could be detached from bureaucratic control by the state. The structural role of the state-supported clergy in society could be reformed. Such social and political alterations could weaken the power of the artificial impediments to the cultivation of the virtues that constitute inwardness.

Kierkegaard's analysis of the novella has more significance for the philosophy of religion and theology than its brevity and modest form suggest. That significance extends beyond the issue of the relation of natural social virtues to Christian *agape*, for it is a subset of the broader matter of the relation of ordinary human experience to religious subjectivity.

Kierkegaard's review offers an alternative to two divergent trajectories in post-Enlightenment religious reflection. Many of the proponents of continuity argue that a depth dimension of human experience serves as a foundation or font from which the various religions arise. Religious subjectivity is an intensification or extension of certain aspects of ordinary human experience. Against this, the advocates of the discontinuity of mundane human experience and religious faith insist that many authoritative religious worldviews contravene all ordinary human hopes and aspirations, generating a qualitatively new and different subjectivity. The significant thing about Kierkegaard's exposition is that human experience and religious subjectivity can relate to one another in neither of these ways.

In distinction from both these views, Kierkegaard implies that some natural forms of attachment are not necessarily inimical to the religious life and may even provide something beneficial to religious subjectivity, but does not construe the religious life as emerging from these natural forms of attachment. Faith does not organically arise from natural virtues. For example, radical love for the neighbor is not an intensification or extension of romantic love, but neither are the two unrelated. Rather than treating the ordinary yearnings of human life as somehow expanding into religious experience, or seeking completion in religious experience, Kierkegaard regards quotidian human virtues as dispositions that can support religious subjectivity. The development of these virtues may be necessary for the blossoming and preservation and growth of faith, hope, and love. In this way social experience need not be dismissed as being entirely inimical to religious subjectivity. Of course, virtues like fidelity, loyalty, responsibility, self-giving, and inwardness can be learned in ways other than certain types of romance or participation in civic communities. Nor must they be acquired chronologically prior to the advent of religious subjectivity. But for Kierkegaard, at least in 1846, they were possible channels of virtue pedagogy.

In 1846–1847 Kierkegaard did not provide a blueprint of a social/political system that would provide such a pedagogy in virtue. He did not outline the contours of a constitutional monarchy, a benevolent despotism, or a people's republic. He did not explicitly show how the conjunctive and disjunctive themes could be integrated. All he did was sketch a few parameters for a culture that wanted to preserve the responsible agency and passionate self-concern of the individual, while it simultaneously nurtured single-mindedness, gratitude for ordinary consolations, loyalty, self-sacrifice, and so on. How that bifocal vision could be implemented was left for the reader to determine. The absence of a ready-made solution should, he hoped, provoke the reader to assume responsibility for her own situation and her own role in it.

# Sigla for Kierkegaard's Works

| | |
|---|---|
| CD | *Christian Discourses* and *The Crisis and a Crisis in the Life of an Actress* |
| CI | *The Concept of Irony* together with "Notes on Schelling's Berlin Lectures," |
| CUP | *Concluding Unscientific Postscript to "Philosophical Fragments,"* 2 vols. |
| EO 1 | *Either/Or: Part I* |
| EO 2 | *Either/Or: Part II* |
| EUD | *Eighteen Upbuilding Discourses* |
| FT | *Fear and Trembling* and *Repetition* |
| KJN 3 | *Kierkegaard's Journals and Notebooks: Vol. 3: Notebooks 1–15* |
| KJN 4 | *Kierkegaard's Journals and Notebooks: Vol. 4: Notebooks NB-NB5* |
| KJN 6 | *Kierkegaard's Journals and Notebooks: Vol. 6, Journals NB11-NB14* |
| KJN 7 | *Kierkegaard's Journals and Notebooks: Vol. 7, Journals NB15-NB20* |
| KJN 8 | *Kierkegaard's Journals and Notebooks: Vol. 8, Journals NB21-NB25* |
| KJN 11.1 | *Kierkegaard's Journals and Notebooks: Vol. 11, pt. 1, Loose Papers, 1830–1843.* |
| KJN 11.2 | *Kierkegaard's Journals and Notebooks: Vol. 11, pt. 2, Loose Papers, 1843–1855.* |
| LD | Letters and Documents |
| PC | *Practice in Christianity* |
| PF | *Philosophical Fragments* and *Johannes Climacus* |
| TM | *"The Moment" and Late Writings* |
| UDVS | *Upbuilding Discourses in Various Spirits* |
| WL | *Works of Love* |

# Bibliography

Because the literature by and about Kierkegaard is vast, the following texts are just a representative sampling.

## Kierkegaard's Texts


Kierkegaard, Søren. *Concluding Unscientific Postscript*. Translated by Howard V. Hong and Edna H. Hong. Princeton, NJ: Princeton University Press, 1992.

Kierkegaard, Søren. *The "Corsair" Affair*. Translated by Howard V. Hong and Edna H. Hong. Princeton, NJ: Princeton University Press, 1982.

Kierkegaard, Søren. *Early Polemical Writings*. Edited and translated by Julia Watkin. Princeton, NJ: Princeton University Press, 1990.

Kierkegaard, Søren. *Eighteen Upbuilding Discourses*. Translated by Howard V. Hong and Edna H. Hong. Princeton, NJ: Princeton University Press, 1990.

Kierkegaard, Søren. *Either/Or*, 2 vols. Translated by Howard V. Hong and Edna H. Hong. Princeton, NJ: Princeton University Press, 1987.

Kierkegaard, Søren. *Kierkegaard's Journals and Notebooks: Vol. 3: Notebooks 1–15*. Edited and translated by Niels Jørgen Cappelørn, Alastair Hannay, Bruce H. Kirmmse, et al. Princeton, NJ: Princeton University Press, 2010.

Kierkegaard, Søren. *Kierkegaard's Journals and Notebooks: Vol.4: Notebooks NB–NB5*. Edited by Niels Jørgen Cappelørn, Alastair Hannay, David Kangas, et al. Princeton, NJ: Princeton University Press, 2011.

Kierkegaard, Søren. *Kierkegaard's Journals and Notebooks: Vol. 7, Journals NB15–NB20*. Edited by Niels Jørgen Cappelørn, Alastair Hannay, Bruce H. Kirmmse, et al. Princeton, NJ: Princeton University Press, 2014.

Kierkegaard, Søren, *Kierkegaard's Journals and Notebooks: Vol. 8, Journals NB21–NB25*. Edited by Niels Jørgen Cappelørn, Alastair Hannay, Bruce H. Kirmmse, et al. Princeton, NJ: Princeton University Press, 2015.

Kierkegaard, Søren. *Kierkegaard's Journals and Notebooks: Vol. 9, Journals NB26–NB30*. Edited by Niels Jørgen Cappelørn, Alastair Hannay, Bruce H. Kirmmse, et al. Princeton, NJ: Princeton University Press, 2017.

Kierkegaard, Søren. *Kierkegaard's Journals and Notebooks: Vol. 10, Journals NB26–NB30*. Edited by Niels Jørgen Cappelørn, Alastair Hannay, Bruce H. Kirmmse, et al. Princeton, NJ: Princeton University Press, 2018.

Kierkegaard, Søren. *Kierkegaard's Journals and Notebooks: Vol. 11, pt. 1, Loose Papers*, 1830–1843. Edited by Niels Jørgen Cappelørn, Alastair Hannay, Bruce H. Kirmmse, et al. Princeton, NJ: Princeton University Press, 2019.

Kierkegaard, Søren. *Kierkegaard's Journals and Notebooks: Vol. 11, pt. 2, Loose Papers*, 1843–1855. Edited by Niels Jørgen Cappelørn, Alastair Hannay, Bruce H. Kirmmse, et al. Princeton, NJ: Princeton University Press, 2020.

Kierkegaard, Søren. *Letters and Documents*. Translated by Hendrik Rosenmeier. Princeton, NJ: Princeton University Press, 1978.

Kierkegaard, Søren. *Two Ages: The Age of Revolution and the Present Age, a Literary Review*. Translated by Howard V. Hong and Edna H. Hong. Princeton, NJ: Princeton University Press, 1978.

Kierkegaard, Søren. *Upbuilding Discourses in Various Spirits*. Translated by Howard V. Hong and Edna H. Hong. Princeton, NJ: Princeton University Press, 1993.

Kierkegaard, Søren. *Works of Love*. Translated by Howard Hong and Edna Hong. Princeton, NJ: Princeton University Press, 1995.

## Other Primary Texts

Grundtvig, Nikolaj. F. S. *The Human Comes First: The Christian Theology of N. S. F. Grundtvig*. Edited and translated by Edward Broadbridge. Aarhus: Aarhus University Press, 2018.

Gyllembourg-Ehrensvärd, Thomasine Christine. *Two Ages*. Edited by Johan I. Heiberg. 1845.

Martensen, Hans Lassen. *Christian Ethics*. Translated by Catherine Spence. Edinburgh: T & T Clark, 1873.

Martensen, Hans Lassen. *"Outline to a System of Moral Philosophy."* In *Between Hegel and Kierkegaard*. Translated by Curtis L. Thompson and David J. Kangas. Atlanta: Scholars Press, 1997, 272–334.

Schlegel, Friedrich. *Friedrich Schlegel's Lucinde and the Fragments*. Translated by Peter Firchow. Minneapolis, MN: University of Minnesota Press, 1971.

## Surveys of Kierkegaard's Thought

Barrett, Lee C. *Eros and Self-Emptying: The Intersections of Kierkegaard and Augustine*. Grand Rapids, MI: Eerdmans, 2013.

Gouwens, David. *Kierkegaard as Religious Thinker*. Cambridge: Cambridge University Press, 1996.

Hannay, Alastair. *Kierkegaard*. New York: Routledge, 1991.

Jamie, Ferreira M. *Kierkegaard*. Chichester: Wiley Blackwell, 2007.

Walsh, Sylvia. *Kierkegaard and Religion: Personality, Character, and Virtue*. Cambridge: Cambridge University Press, 2018.

## Biography and Background


Garff, Joakim. *Søren Kierkegaard: A Biography.* Translated by Bruce H. Kirmmse. Princeton, NJ: Princeton University Press, 2005.

Kirmmse, Bruce H. *Kierkegaard in Golden Age Denmark.* Bloomington: Indiana University Press, 1990.

Nun, Katalin. *Women of the Danish Golden Age: Literature, Theater, and the Emancipation of Women.* Copenhagen: Tusculanum Press, 2013.


## Essay Collections


Buben, Adam, Helms, Eleanor, and Stokes, Patrick. *The Kierkegaardian Mind.* London: Routledge, 2019.

Davenport, John J. and Rudd, Anthony, eds. *Kierkegaard after MacIntyre: Essays on Freedom, Narrative and Virtue.* Chicago, IL: Open Court, 2001.

Edwards, Aaron P. and Gouwens, David, eds. *T&T Clark Companion to the Theology of Kierkegaard.* London: T&T Clark, 2020.

Lippitt, John and Pattison, George, eds. *The Oxford Handbook of Kierkegaard.* Oxford: Oxford University Press, 2013.

Minister, Stephen, Simmons, J. A. and Strawser, Michael, eds. *Kierkegaard's God and the Good Life.* Bloomington, IN: Indiana University Press, 2017.

Stewart, Jon, ed. *A Companion to Kierkegaard.* Oxford: Blackwell, 2015.


## Commentary, Monographs, and Articles


Adorno, Theodor. "On Kierkegaard's Doctrine of Love." *Studies in Philosophy and Social Science,* VIII (1939), pp. 413–429.

Backhouse, Stephen. *Kierkegaard's Critique of Christian Nationalism.* Oxford: Oxford University Press, 2011.

Bukdahl, Jørgen. *Søren Kierkegaard and the Common Man.* Translated by Bruce H. Kirmmse. Eugene, OR: Wipf & Stock, 2001.

Conant, James. "Putting Two and Two Together: Kierkegaard, Wittgenstein, and the Point of View for Their Work as Authors." In *Philosophy and the Grammar of Religious Belief.* Edited by Timothy Tessin and Mario von der Ruhr. London: Palgrave, 1995, 248–331.

Diamond, Cora. *The Realistic Spirit: Wittgenstein, Philosophy, and the Mind.* Cambridge, MA: MIT Press, 1991.

Ferreira, M. Jamie. *Love's Grateful Striving.* Oxford: Oxford University Press, 2001.

Green, Ronald M. and Ellis, Theresa M. "Erotic Love in the Religious Existence-Sphere." In *International Kierkegaard Commentary 16: Works of*

*Love*. Edited by Robert L. Perkins. Macon, GA: Mercer University Press, 1999, 339–367.

Krishek, Sharon. *Kierkegaard on Faith and Love*. Cambridge: Cambridge University Press, 2015.

Lippitt, John. "Kierkegaard and the Problem of Special Relationships: Ferreira, Krishek, and the 'God Filter.'" *International Journal for Philosophy of Religion*, 72 (3)(2012):177–197.

Løgstrup, Knud Ejler. *Opgør med Kierkegaard*. Copenhagen: Gyldendal, 2005.

Marandiuc, Natalia. *The Goodness of Home*. Oxford: Oxford University Press, 2018.

Mulhall, Stephen. *Faith and Reason*. London: Duckworth, 1994.

Sløk, Johannes. *Da Kierkegaard tav: Fra forfatterskab til kirkestorm*. Copenhagen: Reitzel, 1980.

Søltoft, Pia. "On God, Passion, Faith, and Falling in Love." In *Kierkegaard's God and the Good Life*. Edited by J. Aaron Simmons Stephen Minister and Michael Strawser. Bloomington, IN: Indiana University Press, 2017, 31–45.

Stan, Leo. *Selfhood and Otherness in Kierkegaard's Authorship: A Heterological Investigation*. Lanham, MD: Lexington, 2017.

Watts, Daniel. "Love's Telos: Kierkegaard's Critique of Preferential Love." In *The Philosophy of Love in the Past, Present, and Future*. Edited by Natasha McKeever, Joe Saunders, and André Grahle. London: Routledge, 2021, 54–72.

Wende, Matias Tapia. "The Concept of State in Kierkegaard's *Papers*." In *Kierkegaard Studies Yearbook, 2021*. Edited by Heiko Schulz, Jon Stewart, and Karl Verstringe. Berlin: De Gruyter, 2021, 105–136.

# Philosophy of Søren Kierkegaard

Rick Anthony Furtak
*Colorado College*

Rick Anthony Furtak is Associate Professor of Philosophy at Colorado College and past President of the Søren Kierkegaard Society (for calendar years 2013–2014). He has published two books and over twenty essays on Kierkegaard's work, including *Wisdom in Love: Kierkegaard and the Ancient Quest for Emotional Integrity* (2005) and *Kierkegaard's 'Concluding Unscientific Postscript': A Critical Guide* (2010), along with the co-edited *Kierkegaard and the Poetry of the Gospel* (2025). He has contributed to each of the *Cambridge Critical Guides* on Kierkegaard's writings, and has dozens of other philosophical and poetic publications. He is also an Editorial Board Member for *New Kierkegaard Research* and founding Book Series Co-Editor for *Bloomsbury Studies in Philosophy and Poetry*. His other recent books include *Love, Subjectivity, and Truth* (2023).

## About the Series

This series offers concise and structured introductions to all aspects of the philosophy of Søren Kierkegaard. Some Elements are organized around particular themes, while others are devoted to specific Kierkegaardian texts. Both well-established and emerging scholars contribute to the series, combining decades of expertise with new and different perspectives.

For EU product safety concerns, contact us at Calle de José Abascal, 56–1°,
28003 Madrid, Spain or eugpsr@cambridge.org.